```
MW00911390
```

THE
ORIGINAL
INTERNET
ADDRESS
BOOK

THE ORIGINAL INTERNET ADDRESS BOOK

Created by The Mesa Group

PRENTICE HALL
Englewood Cliffs, New Jersey 07632

Library of Congress Cataloging-in-Publication Data

The Original Internet address book / Mesa Group.
      p.   cm.
  ISBN 0-13-260431-0 (paper)
  ISBN 0-13-269887-0 (paper 10 pack)
  1. Internet (Computer networks)--Directories. I. MESA
Group (Firm)
ZA4201.075 1996   96-32050
025.04--dc20   CIP

© 1996 by The Mesa Group

ATTENTION: CORPORATIONS AND SCHOOLS

Prentice Hall books are available at quantity discounts with
bulk purchase for educational, business, or sales promotional use. For information, please write to: Prentice Hall
Career & Personal Development Special Sales, 113 Sylvan
Avenue, Englewood Cliffs, NJ 07632. Please supply: title of
book, ISBN number, quantity, how the book will be used,
date needed.

PRENTICE HALL
Career & Personal Development
Englewood Cliffs, NJ 07632
A Simon & Schuster Company

On the World Wide Web at http://www.phdirect.com

Printed in the United States of America

10 9 8 7 6 5 4 3

ISBN 0-13-260431-0 (paper)
ISBN 0-13-269887-0 (paper 10 pack)

Prentice Hall International (UK) Limited, *London*
Prentice Hall of Australia Pty. Limited, *Sydney*
Prentice Hall Canada, Inc., *Toronto*
Prentice Hall Hispanoamericana, S.A., *Mexico*
Prentice Hall of India Private Limited, *New Delhi*
Prentice Hall of Japan, Inc., *Tokyo*
Simon & Schuster Asia Pte. Ltd., *Singapore*
Editora Prentice Hall do Brasil, Ltda., *Rio de Janeiro*

INTRODUCTION

The book you hold in your hand began life as a 12-page promotional booklet for our advertising agency. We thought it would fill a genuine need for our clients and friends. We also thought it would show our commitment to this phenomena called the Internet. And it sounded like fun!

It turned out to be all of the above and more. Everyone seemed amazed that nothing like this book existed. People asked for customized versions for their businesses. Our good friend, agent, book packager and former publisher Tony Seidl thought it would make a great book. And Gene Brissie at Prentice Hall agreed!

When we created this edition, we added a section on search engines, room for phone or fax numbers, and a line to put keyword addresses from the online services. In addition, we expanded the available listings from the original 12 pages.

The result is a book we hope you find truly useful. Anyone who "surfs" the Net for business or pleasure knows how easy it is to bookmark a location when you're on your computer. That's easy. The problem is remembering all the sites you discover when you're reading a book, newspaper or magazine, listening to the radio or watching television. It's the same dilemma when someone tells you "you have to check out this site at http://www. etc., etc., etc."

Eventually we found ourselves overwhelmed with torn-out stories, ads and little slips of paper with URL addresses, keywords and e-mail addresses. We knew there had to be a better way, so one day, in sheer frustration, we created "The Original Internet Address Book©".

You use this book exactly the way you use any address book. Just keep it handy (hint:

we designed it to fit into a small space like a pocket or pocketbook). Now, when you read or hear about a Web site or newsgroup, or someone gives you an e-mail address, or you see something interesting on one of the online services like AOL, CompuServe or Prodigy, just write it down. That's right, write it down. Now this may not sound very high tech, but it's really quite practical. Soon you'll have a list of Web sites, newsgroups, key words and e-mail addresses all in one place.

Now you may be wondering, "What do I do with these addresses after I've put them into my computer?" Frankly, we did too. But it didn't take long to discover other uses for this book. For example, when you're working on someone else's computer, you've got your "bookmarks" with you. Or you get home and find the bookmark you made in the office isn't doing you much good at ten o'clock at night because it's still in the office. Now it's also at home.

But our favorite use for the "post-bookmark period" is when you're talking to someone about the great site you saw on the Internet, or the really interesting news group you're in, and they want to know where to find it. Now you just whip out your "Original Internet Address Book" and glibly say: "Oh, it's at http://........" Get the idea?

We hope you find our book useful and fun to use. And we hope you'll share your thoughts on any way we can make it even better in the future. Just e-mail us at

mike@mesagrp.com.

Michael Sloser
Chairman/CEO, The Mesa Group
September, 1996

A FEW WORDS
ABOUT SEARCH ENGINES

A search engine is a fancy word for a site on the Internet that helps you find other Internet sites. Think of them as a cross between phone books and information operators. There are dozens of them, with new ones cropping up every month. Some have cute names like Yahoo and Deja News, Excite and Jump City, Archie and Veronica. Others sound a bit technical, like CUSI and Lycos. Fear not. They're all there to help you and me find places to go on the Internet.

Most people are really interested in two major sections of the Internet. One is the place everyone is talking about, namely the World Wide Web. It's where seemingly everyone has a site, or as they're usually called, a "home page." Home pages are colorful, often interactive, and thanks to new technology, can give you real time audio, video, and animation. When you see a URL (Uniform Resource Locator), or address, that has the letters www after http (most URLs start that way), you can be sure you're going to the World Wide Web. They appear in magazines and newspapers, in books and increasingly on radio and TV. Now you have a place to write them down!

This is as good a time as ever to remind you that you have to type in every letter, slash, period, comma, etc. to get to an address. For reasons that are a mystery to most of us, leaving out the smallest details will get you the dreaded "unable to locate" message.

Some Web sites are good, many just average, and a sizable number are simply terrible or boring, or both. But with over 100,000 Internet sites as of this writing, you need a way to find the sites and the subjects that appeal to you. And the way to do all of this is to understand search engines. Some simply list sites that are out there, often by subject. Think of a telephone book. Others ask you what you want, like a telephone operator. Many do both.

It's good to know where some of these search engines are so we decided to select a sampling of them for this address book. Whether you're looking for computer books, personal finance, car manufacturers or newspapers on the net, search engines will make life easier and the net far more enjoyable to use. By the way, most also have a "what's new" and "what's cool" section. Check them out.

The other part of the Internet many people go to is called Usenet. You'll frequently see this referred to as newsgroups. They're broken down by special interests. Some are quite useful, some worthless, and a few simply bizarre. Since they can be confusing to use, search engines like Deja News or the Usenet Info Center home page will help you find the groups that fit your interests.

Many people use newsgroups to develop their business and personal interests. They can be a great source of information on starting a new business, on travel tips from people who've gone where you want to go, and for medical advice shared freely and openly. Others are just great places to share your thoughts (or ventilate a few) on topics that interest you. Whatever your goal, these search engines will help you find the newsgroups that are right for you.

Generally we find that most people use a small handful of search engines. But with new ones coming along, and existing ones upgrading their services, we think it's good to know as many as possible. While this list is not complete, it will give you ample resources to help you find the proverbial needle in a cyberspace haystack.

SOME OF OUR FAVORITE SEARCH ENGINES ON THE Internet

YAHOO
(http://www.yahoo.com)

Started by two resourceful students at Stanford, Yahoo has become one of the most popular search engines on the Internet. In addition to listing new, cool and popular sites, it has listings by categories, searches for specific locations and Reuters News Headlines if you're keeping up with the news. Yahoo covers the Web, gopher sites, FTP (places that let you download files from) as well as selected newsgroups. It's well-run, up-to-date and easy-to-use. Need we say more?

DEJA NEWS
(http://www.dejanews.com)

Say you're looking for people who own small retail stores to share your tales of woe with. Look no further. Just type in a description of what you want and you'll get a list of current chat picked up from key phrases. Click on the interesting ones and you can see which groups are right for you. Of course there is a help section. Of course we needed it.

THE Internet SLEUTH
(http://www.intbc.com:80/sleuth/sleuth.html)

They claim to cover the top 5% of the Internet. Who are we to argue? What we really liked was that they give you a great list of other Internet Search Engines. In other words, if you can't find what you want here, you can go to a nice list of additional Search Engines to check out. Sort of like using this book.

INFOSEEK
(http://www2.infoseek.com)

Fast, accurate and comprehensive—that's what they say. Judging from our visit there, it is. But this is really two search engines in one. The free side searches all the usual suspects. But if you go to the "Professional" section, you'll find a subscription service that checks wire services, business periodicals, public and commercial databases and more. If the price is right, it may be some of the cheapest business research around.

EXCITE
(http://www.excite.com)

You've got to love it for the name alone. They say they search over 1.4 million Web pages, have more than 1 million articles from over 10,000 newsgroups, have Web site reviews, news and cartoons, and let you search Usenet classified ads. You just might find yourself actually excited (sorry for the pun!) by this Search Engine.

ALTA VISTA
(http://altavista.digital.com)

This is a new entry from the folks at Digital Equipment Corporation. What do we hear about it other than it's new? Well it's supposed to be fast, claims the largest Web index around (8 billion words found in over 16 million Web pages) plus it delivers over 13,000 newsgroups updated in real time. Who could ask for anything more?

JUMP CITY
(http://www.jumpcity.com)

You've got to love a search engine that starts with "ladiesandgentlemen,thecaptainhas- turned onthenosmokinglight" etc. Lots of color and graphics, it lets you search either by key- word or by subject matter. They publish books and if you have keywords from their books, you don't need a URL. Another nice feature is a review of sites they list. There's also a news link but we've had little success with it. Other than that, we're impressed.

FEMINA
(http://www.femina.com)

They say at least 1/3 of the people using the Net are women. So wouldn't it be nice if they had their own search engine? Well they do, and it's loaded with content, from art and cul- ture to sports and writing. You can also do a subject or title search. Plus there are links to other sites serving women.

WEB NEWS
(http://twinbrook.cis.uab.edu:70/webNews.80)

All announcements of newly-created Web sites posted to Newsgroups by Web site developers are here. Not only can you find everything "out there," but you also have links to the URL's in question. Leave youself plenty of time, since this could keep you busy for hours.

USENET INFO CENTER
(http://sunsite.unc.edu/usenet-i/)

They call themselves "your source for informa- tion on Usenet and its newsgroups." In addition to FAQs (Frequently Asked Questions), they give you help on using Usenet, let you browse through Usenet groups, search for a particular Usenet group, and even point you to other Usenet indexes and services. Definitely a place to go if you're heading to Usenet.

SEARCH.COM
(http://www.search.com)

Brought to you by the savvy folks at C/Net, this is a search vehicle of search vehicles. It lets you use a number of the popular search engines from their site. In addition they give you search engines by popular categories. In fact they claim to have 250 ways to search the net. Now if that's not cool enough, you can custom-tailor the site to your taste. Definitely worth a visit!

HOTBOT
(http://www.hotbot.com)

Just when we thought there couldn't be yet another new search engine, and were ready to put this book to bed, up pops Hotbot. A joint venture of Hotwired and Inktomi, they claim to link work stations together to act like a super-computer and be able to search over 50 million pages. More impressive is their ability to qualify a search by date of the site posting, domain type like .com or .edu and more. We suspect we'll be hearing a lot about them.

NAME: ABC NEWS RadioNet
URL: http://www.abcradionet.com

NAME: Adobe Systems Incorporated
URL: http://www.adobe.com

NAME: Amazon.com Books
URL: http://www.amazon.com

NAME: American Airlines
URL: http://www.americanair.com

NAME: American Booksellers Association
URL: http://www.ambook.org/bookweb/aba

NAME: American Newspaper Network
URL: http://www.amnewsnet.com

NAME: American Stock Exchange
URL: http://www.amex.com

NAME: Antiquarian Booksellers' Association of America
URL: http://www.abaa-booknet.com

NAME: Apple Computer Company
URL: http://www.apple.com

NAME: AT&T
URL: http://www.att.com

NAME_____

E-MAIL ADDRESS _____

URL: http:// _____

KEYWORD _____

PHONE/FAX _____

NAME_____

E-MAIL ADDRESS _____

URL: http:// _____

KEYWORD _____

PHONE/FAX _____

NAME _____

E-MAIL ADDRESS _____

URL: http://_____

KEYWORD _____

PHONE/FAX _____

NAME _____

E-MAIL ADDRESS _____

URL: http://_____

KEYWORD _____

PHONE/FAX _____

NAME _____

E-MAIL ADDRESS _____

URL: http://_____

KEYWORD _____

PHONE/FAX _____

NAME _____

E-MAIL ADDRESS _____

URL: http://_____

KEYWORD _____

PHONE/FAX _____

NAME _____

E-MAIL ADDRESS _____

URL: http://_____

KEYWORD _____

PHONE/FAX _____

NAME _____

E-MAIL ADDRESS _____

URL: http:// _____

KEYWORD _____

PHONE/FAX _____

NAME _____

E-MAIL ADDRESS _____

URL: http:// _____

KEYWORD _____

PHONE/FAX _____

NAME _____

E-MAIL ADDRESS _____

URL: http:// _____

KEYWORD _____

PHONE/FAX _____

NAME _____

E-MAIL ADDRESS _____

URL: http:// _____

KEYWORD _____

PHONE/FAX _____

NAME _____

E-MAIL ADDRESS _____

URL: http:// _____

KEYWORD _____

PHONE/FAX _____

NAME _____

E-MAIL ADDRESS _____

URL: http:// _____

KEYWORD _____

PHONE/FAX _____

NAME _____

E-MAIL ADDRESS _____

URL: http:// _____

KEYWORD _____

PHONE/FAX _____

NAME _____

E-MAIL ADDRESS _____

URL: http:// _____

KEYWORD _____

PHONE/FAX _____

NAME _____

E-MAIL ADDRESS _____

URL: http:// _____

KEYWORD _____

PHONE/FAX _____

NAME _____

E-MAIL ADDRESS _____

URL: http:// _____

KEYWORD _____

PHONE/FAX _____

NAME _____

E-MAIL ADDRESS _____

URL: http:// _____

KEYWORD _____

PHONE/FAX _____

NAME _____

E-MAIL ADDRESS _____

URL: http:// _____

KEYWORD _____

PHONE/FAX _____

NAME _____

E-MAIL ADDRESS _____

URL: http:// _____

KEYWORD _____

PHONE/FAX _____

NAME _____

E-MAIL ADDRESS _____

URL: http:// _____

KEYWORD _____

PHONE/FAX _____

NAME _____

E-MAIL ADDRESS _____

URL: http:// _____

KEYWORD _____

PHONE/FAX _____

NAME _____

E-MAIL ADDRESS _____

URL: http:// _____

KEYWORD _____

PHONE/FAX _____

NAME _____

E-MAIL ADDRESS _____

URL: http:// _____

KEYWORD _____

PHONE/FAX _____

NAME _____

E-MAIL ADDRESS _____

URL: http:// _____

KEYWORD _____

PHONE/FAX _____

NAME _____

E-MAIL ADDRESS _____

URL: http:// _____

KEYWORD _____

PHONE/FAX _____

NAME _____

E-MAIL ADDRESS _____

URL: http:// _____

KEYWORD _____

PHONE/FAX _____

NAME: Big Yellow
URL: http://www.bigyellow.com

NAME: BizCafe Mall
URL: http://www.pwgroup.com/mall

NAME: BMW Automobiles
URL: http://www.bmwusa.com

NAME Bookwire
URL: http://www.bookwire.com

NAME: Boeing
URL: http://www.boeing.com

NAME: Borders Books and Music
URL: http://www.borders.com/borders

NAME: British American Chamber of Commerce
URL: http://bacc.conpro.org

NAME: Buick
URL: http://www.buick.com

NAME Business World
URL: http://www.dks.com/businessworld

NAME Buzznet Magazine
URL: http://www.buzznet.com

NAME _____

E-MAIL ADDRESS _____

URL: http:// _____

KEYWORD _____

PHONE/FAX _____

NAME _____

E-MAIL ADDRESS _____

URL: http:// _____

KEYWORD _____

PHONE/FAX _____

NAME _____

E-MAIL ADDRESS _____

URL: http:// _____

KEYWORD _____

PHONE/FAX _____

NAME _____

E-MAIL ADDRESS _____

URL: http:// _____

KEYWORD _____

PHONE/FAX _____

NAME _____

E-MAIL ADDRESS _____

URL: http:// _____

KEYWORD _____

PHONE/FAX _____

NAME _____

E-MAIL ADDRESS _____

URL: http:// _____

KEYWORD _____

PHONE/FAX _____

NAME _____

E-MAIL ADDRESS _____

URL: http:// _____

KEYWORD _____

PHONE/FAX _____

NAME _____

E-MAIL ADDRESS _____

URL: http:// _____

KEYWORD _____

PHONE/FAX _____

NAME _____

E-MAIL ADDRESS _____

URL: http:// _____

KEYWORD _____

PHONE/FAX _____

NAME _____

E-MAIL ADDRESS _____

URL: http:// _____

KEYWORD _____

PHONE/FAX _____

NAME _____

E-MAIL ADDRESS _____

URL: http:// _____

KEYWORD _____

PHONE/FAX _____

NAME _____

E-MAIL ADDRESS _____

URL: http:// _____

KEYWORD _____

PHONE/FAX _____

NAME _____

E-MAIL ADDRESS _____

URL: http:// _____

KEYWORD _____

PHONE/FAX _____

NAME _____

E-MAIL ADDRESS _____

URL: http:// _____

KEYWORD _____

PHONE/FAX _____

NAME _____

E-MAIL ADDRESS _____

URL: http:// _____

KEYWORD _____

PHONE/FAX _____

NAME _____

E-MAIL ADDRESS _____

URL: http:// _____

KEYWORD _____

PHONE/FAX _____

NAME _____

E-MAIL ADDRESS _____

URL: http:// _____

KEYWORD _____

PHONE/FAX _____

NAME _____

E-MAIL ADDRESS _____

URL: http:// _____

KEYWORD _____

PHONE/FAX _____

NAME _____

E-MAIL ADDRESS _____

URL: http:// _____

KEYWORD _____

PHONE/FAX _____

NAME _____

E-MAIL ADDRESS _____

URL: http:// _____

KEYWORD _____

PHONE/FAX _____

NAME _____

E-MAIL ADDRESS _____

URL: http:// _____

KEYWORD _____

PHONE/FAX _____

NAME _____

E-MAIL ADDRESS _____

URL: http:// _____

KEYWORD _____

PHONE/FAX _____

NAME _____

E-MAIL ADDRESS _____

URL: http:// _____

KEYWORD _____

PHONE/FAX _____

NAME _____

E-MAIL ADDRESS _____

URL: http:// _____

KEYWORD _____

PHONE/FAX _____

NAME _____

E-MAIL ADDRESS _____

URL: http:// _____

KEYWORD _____

PHONE/FAX _____

NAME _____

E-MAIL ADDRESS _____

URL: http:// _____

KEYWORD _____

PHONE/FAX _____

NAME _____

E-MAIL ADDRESS _____

URL: http:// _____

KEYWORD _____

PHONE/FAX _____

NAME: C/Net
URL: http://www.cnet.com

NAME: Cadillac
URL: http://www.cadillac.com

NAME: Career Path: employment ads from six major cities
URL: http://www.careerpath.com

NAME: CBS-TV
URL: http://www.cbs.com

NAME: Chevrolet
URL: http://www.chevrolet.com

NAME: Chrysler
URL: http://www.chryslercars.com

NAME: CNBC
URL: http://www.cnbc.com

NAME: CNN
URL: http://www.cnn.com

NAME: Comedy Central
URL: http://www.comcentral.com

NAME: The Copyright Website
URL: http://www.benedict.com

NAME _____

E-MAIL ADDRESS _____

URL: http:// _____

KEYWORD _____

PHONE/FAX _____

NAME _____

E-MAIL ADDRESS _____

URL: http:// _____

KEYWORD _____

PHONE/FAX _____

NAME _____

E-MAIL ADDRESS _____

URL: http:// _____

KEYWORD _____

PHONE/FAX _____

NAME _____

E-MAIL ADDRESS _____

URL: http:// _____

KEYWORD _____

PHONE/FAX _____

NAME _____

E-MAIL ADDRESS _____

URL: http:// _____

KEYWORD _____

PHONE/FAX _____

NAME _____

E-MAIL ADDRESS _____

URL: http:// _____

KEYWORD _____

PHONE/FAX _____

NAME _____

E-MAIL ADDRESS _____

URL: http:// _____

KEYWORD _____

PHONE/FAX _____

NAME _____

E-MAIL ADDRESS _____

URL: http:// _____

KEYWORD _____

PHONE/FAX _____

NAME _____

E-MAIL ADDRESS _____

URL: http:// _____

KEYWORD _____

PHONE/FAX _____

NAME _____

E-MAIL ADDRESS _____

URL: http:// _____

KEYWORD _____

PHONE/FAX _____

NAME _____

E-MAIL ADDRESS _____

URL: http:// _____

KEYWORD _____

PHONE/FAX _____

NAME _____

E-MAIL ADDRESS _____

URL: http:// _____

KEYWORD _____

PHONE/FAX _____

NAME _____

E-MAIL ADDRESS _____

URL: http:// _____

KEYWORD _____

PHONE/FAX _____

NAME _____

E-MAIL ADDRESS _____

URL: http:// _____

KEYWORD _____

PHONE/FAX _____

NAME _____

E-MAIL ADDRESS _____

URL: http:// _____

KEYWORD _____

PHONE/FAX _____

NAME _____

E-MAIL ADDRESS _____

URL: http:// _____

KEYWORD _____

PHONE/FAX _____

NAME _____

E-MAIL ADDRESS _____

URL: http:// _____

KEYWORD _____

PHONE/FAX _____

NAME _____

E-MAIL ADDRESS _____

URL: http:// _____

KEYWORD _____

PHONE/FAX _____

NAME _____

E-MAIL ADDRESS _____

URL: http:// _____

KEYWORD _____

PHONE/FAX_____

NAME _____

E-MAIL ADDRESS _____

URL: http:// _____

KEYWORD _____

PHONE/FAX_____

NAME _____

E-MAIL ADDRESS _____

URL: http:// _____

KEYWORD _____

PHONE/FAX_____

NAME _____

E-MAIL ADDRESS _____

URL: http:// _____

KEYWORD _____

PHONE/FAX_____

NAME _____

E-MAIL ADDRESS _____

URL: http:// _____

KEYWORD _____

PHONE/FAX _____

NAME _____

E-MAIL ADDRESS _____

URL: http:// _____

KEYWORD _____

PHONE/FAX _____

NAME _____

E-MAIL ADDRESS _____

URL: http:// _____

KEYWORD _____

PHONE/FAX _____

NAME _____

E-MAIL ADDRESS _____

URL: http:// _____

KEYWORD _____

PHONE/FAX _____

NAME _____

E-MAIL ADDRESS _____

URL: http:// _____

KEYWORD _____

PHONE/FAX _____

NAME: Dallas Morning News
URL: http://www.pic.net/tdmn/tdmn.html

NAME: DealerNet
URL: http://www.dealerNet.com

NAME: Debt Calculator
URL: http://uclc.com/uclc/debt.html

D

NAME: Digital Future Coalition
URL: http://www.ari.net/dfc

NAME: Dilbert Zone
URL: http://www.unitedmedia.com/comics/dilbert

NAME: Discovery/Learning Channel
URL: http://www.discovery.com

NAME: Dodge
URL: http://www.4adodge.com

NAME: Dream Jobs
URL: http://www.hotwired.com/dreamjobs

NAME: Dreyfus
URL: http://www.dreyfus.com/funds

NAME _____

E-MAIL ADDRESS _____

URL: http:// _____

KEYWORD _____

PHONE/FAX _____

NAME _____

E-MAIL ADDRESS _____

URL: http:// _____

KEYWORD _____

PHONE/FAX _____

NAME _____

E-MAIL ADDRESS _____

URL: http:// _____

KEYWORD _____

PHONE/FAX _____

NAME _____

E-MAIL ADDRESS _____

URL: http:// _____

KEYWORD _____

PHONE/FAX _____

NAME _____

E-MAIL ADDRESS _____

URL: http:// _____

KEYWORD _____

PHONE/FAX _____

NAME _____

E-MAIL ADDRESS _____

URL: http:// _____

KEYWORD _____

PHONE/FAX _____

NAME _____

E-MAIL ADDRESS _____

URL: http:// _____

KEYWORD _____

PHONE/FAX _____

NAME _____

E-MAIL ADDRESS _____

URL: http:// _____

KEYWORD _____

PHONE/FAX _____

NAME _____

E-MAIL ADDRESS _____

URL: http:// _____

KEYWORD _____

PHONE/FAX _____

NAME _____

E-MAIL ADDRESS _____

URL: http:// _____

KEYWORD _____

PHONE/FAX _____

NAME _____

E-MAIL ADDRESS _____

URL: http:// _____

KEYWORD _____

PHONE/FAX _____

NAME _____

E-MAIL ADDRESS _____

URL: http:// _____

KEYWORD _____

PHONE/FAX _____

NAME _____

E-MAIL ADDRESS _____

URL: http:// _____

KEYWORD _____

PHONE/FAX _____

NAME _____

E-MAIL ADDRESS _____

URL: http:// _____

KEYWORD _____

PHONE/FAX _____

NAME _____

E-MAIL ADDRESS _____

URL: http:// _____

KEYWORD _____

PHONE/FAX _____

NAME _____

E-MAIL ADDRESS _____

URL: http:// _____

KEYWORD _____

PHONE/FAX _____

NAME _____

E-MAIL ADDRESS _____

URL: http:// _____

KEYWORD _____

PHONE/FAX _____

NAME _____

E-MAIL ADDRESS _____

URL: http:// _____

KEYWORD _____

PHONE/FAX _____

NAME _____

E-MAIL ADDRESS _____

URL: http:// _____

KEYWORD _____

PHONE/FAX _____

NAME _____

E-MAIL ADDRESS _____

URL: http:// _____

KEYWORD _____

PHONE/FAX _____

NAME _____

E-MAIL ADDRESS _____

URL: http:// _____

KEYWORD _____

PHONE/FAX _____

NAME _____

E-MAIL ADDRESS _____

URL: http:// _____

KEYWORD _____

PHONE/FAX _____

NAME _____

E-MAIL ADDRESS _____

URL: http:// _____

KEYWORD _____

PHONE/FAX _____

NAME _____

E-MAIL ADDRESS _____

URL: http:// _____

KEYWORD _____

PHONE/FAX _____

NAME _____

E-MAIL ADDRESS _____

URL: http:// _____

KEYWORD _____

PHONE/FAX _____

NAME _____

E-MAIL ADDRESS _____

URL: http:// _____

KEYWORD _____

PHONE/FAX _____

NAME _____

E-MAIL ADDRESS _____

URL: http:// _____

KEYWORD _____

PHONE/FAX _____

NAME: Eagle Cars
URL: http://www.eaglecars.com

NAME: EDNET–Employment Opportunities for Educators
URL: http://pages.prodigy.com/CA/luca52a/bagley.html

NAME: Editor & Publisher Interactive
URL: http://www.mediainfo.com

NAME: Egghead Software
URL: http://www.egghead.com

E

NAME: Electronic Telegraph (British newspaper)
URL: http://www.telegraph.co.uk

NAME: The Entrepreneur Network
URL: http://www.bizserve.com/ten

NAME: Entrepreneur Weekly
URL: http://www.valleynet.net/~eweekly

NAME: European Market Entry
URL: http://www.sme.com/lukas.consulting

NAME: The EvangeList
URL: http://www.evangelist.macaddict.com

NAME: EXPOguide
URL: http://www.expoguide.com

NAME _____

E-MAIL ADDRESS _____

URL: http:// _____

KEYWORD _____

PHONE/FAX _____

NAME _____

E-MAIL ADDRESS _____

URL: http:// _____

KEYWORD _____

PHONE/FAX _____

NAME _____

E-MAIL ADDRESS _____

URL: http:// _____

KEYWORD _____

PHONE/FAX* _____

NAME _____

E-MAIL ADDRESS _____

URL: http:// _____

KEYWORD _____

PHONE/FAX _____

NAME _____

E-MAIL ADDRESS _____

URL: http:// _____

KEYWORD _____

PHONE/FAX _____

NAME _____

E-MAIL ADDRESS _____

URL: http:// _____

KEYWORD _____

PHONE/FAX _____

NAME _____

E-MAIL ADDRESS _____

URL: http:// _____

KEYWORD _____

PHONE/FAX _____

NAME _____

E-MAIL ADDRESS _____

URL: http:// _____

KEYWORD _____

PHONE/FAX _____

NAME _____

E-MAIL ADDRESS _____

URL: http:// _____

KEYWORD _____

PHONE/FAX _____

NAME _____

E-MAIL ADDRESS _____

URL: http:// _____

KEYWORD _____

PHONE/FAX _____

NAME _____

E-MAIL ADDRESS _____

URL: http:// _____

KEYWORD _____

PHONE/FAX _____

NAME _____

E-MAIL ADDRESS _____

URL: http:// _____

KEYWORD _____

PHONE/FAX _____

NAME _____

E-MAIL ADDRESS _____

URL: http:// _____

KEYWORD _____

PHONE/FAX _____

NAME _____

E-MAIL ADDRESS _____

URL: http:// _____

KEYWORD _____

PHONE/FAX _____

NAME _____

E-MAIL ADDRESS _____

URL: http:// _____

KEYWORD _____

PHONE/FAX _____

NAME _____

E-MAIL ADDRESS _____

URL: http:// _____

KEYWORD _____

PHONE/FAX _____

NAME _____

E-MAIL ADDRESS _____

URL: http:// _____

KEYWORD _____

PHONE/FAX _____

NAME _____

E-MAIL ADDRESS _____

URL: http:// _____

KEYWORD _____

PHONE/FAX _____

NAME _____

E-MAIL ADDRESS _____

URL: http:// _____

KEYWORD _____

PHONE/FAX _____

NAME _____

E-MAIL ADDRESS _____

URL: http:// _____

KEYWORD _____

PHONE/FAX _____

NAME _____

E-MAIL ADDRESS _____

URL: http:// _____

KEYWORD _____

PHONE/FAX _____

NAME _____

E-MAIL ADDRESS _____

URL: http:// _____

KEYWORD _____

PHONE/FAX _____

NAME _____

E-MAIL ADDRESS _____

URL: http:// _____

KEYWORD _____

PHONE/FAX _____

NAME _____

E-MAIL ADDRESS _____

URL: http:// _____

KEYWORD _____

PHONE/FAX _____

NAME _____

E-MAIL ADDRESS _____

URL: http:// _____

KEYWORD _____

PHONE/FAX _____

NAME _____

E-MAIL ADDRESS _____

URL: http:// _____

KEYWORD _____

PHONE/FAX _____

NAME _____

E-MAIL ADDRESS _____

URL: http:// _____

KEYWORD _____

PHONE/FAX _____

NAME Federal Government
URL: http://www.fedworld.gov

NAME: FEDEX
URL: http://www.fedex.com

NAME: Fidelity Investments
URL: http://www.fid-inv.com

NAME: Financial Resource Guide
URL: http://www.libertynet.org/~beausang

NAME: FODORS
URL: http://www.fodors.com

NAME: Form for Mortgage Payment Query
URL: http://ibc.wust1.edu/mort.html

NAME: France World Contacts Web
URL: http://www.francecontacts.com/bonjour.html

NAME: Franchise Net
URL: http://www.frannet.com

NAME: FTD Internet
URL: http://www.ftd.com

NAME: FX Cable Network
URL: http://www.fxnetworks.com

NAME _____

E-MAIL ADDRESS _____

URL: http:// _____

KEYWORD _____

PHONE/FAX_____

NAME _____

E-MAIL ADDRESS _____

URL: http:// _____

KEYWORD _____

PHONE/FAX_____

NAME _____

E-MAIL ADDRESS _____

URL: http:// _____

KEYWORD _____

PHONE/FAX _____

NAME _____

E-MAIL ADDRESS _____

URL: http:// _____

KEYWORD _____

PHONE/FAX _____

NAME _____

E-MAIL ADDRESS _____

URL: http:// _____

KEYWORD _____

PHONE/FAX _____

NAME _____

E-MAIL ADDRESS _____

URL: http:// _____

KEYWORD _____

PHONE/FAX _____

NAME _____

E-MAIL ADDRESS _____

URL: http:// _____

KEYWORD _____

PHONE/FAX _____

NAME _____

E-MAIL ADDRESS _____

URL: http:// _____

KEYWORD _____

PHONE/FAX _____

NAME _____

E-MAIL ADDRESS _____

URL: http:// _____

KEYWORD _____

PHONE/FAX _____

NAME _____

E-MAIL ADDRESS _____

URL: http:// _____

KEYWORD _____

PHONE/FAX _____

NAME _____

E-MAIL ADDRESS _____

URL: http:// _____

KEYWORD _____

PHONE/FAX _____

NAME _____

E-MAIL ADDRESS _____

URL: http:// _____

KEYWORD _____

PHONE/FAX _____

NAME _____

E-MAIL ADDRESS _____

URL: http:// _____

KEYWORD _____

PHONE/FAX _____

NAME _____

E-MAIL ADDRESS _____

URL: http:// _____

KEYWORD _____

PHONE/FAX _____

NAME _____

E-MAIL ADDRESS _____

URL: http:// _____

KEYWORD _____

PHONE/FAX _____

NAME _____

E-MAIL ADDRESS _____

URL: http:// _____

KEYWORD _____

PHONE/FAX _____

NAME _____

E-MAIL ADDRESS _____

URL: http:// _____

KEYWORD _____

PHONE/FAX _____

NAME _____

E-MAIL ADDRESS _____

URL: http:// _____

KEYWORD _____

PHONE/FAX _____

NAME _____

E-MAIL ADDRESS _____

URL: http:// _____

KEYWORD _____

PHONE/FAX _____

NAME _____

E-MAIL ADDRESS _____

URL: http:// _____

KEYWORD _____

PHONE/FAX _____

NAME _____

E-MAIL ADDRESS _____

URL: http:// _____

KEYWORD _____

PHONE/FAX _____

NAME _____

E-MAIL ADDRESS _____

URL: http:// _____

KEYWORD _____

PHONE/FAX _____

NAME _____

E-MAIL ADDRESS _____

URL: http:// _____

KEYWORD _____

PHONE/FAX _____

NAME _____

E-MAIL ADDRESS _____

URL: http:// _____

KEYWORD _____

PHONE/FAX _____

NAME _____

E-MAIL ADDRESS _____

URL: http:// _____

KEYWORD _____

PHONE/FAX _____

NAME _____

E-MAIL ADDRESS _____

URL: http:// _____

KEYWORD _____

PHONE/FAX _____

NAME _____

E-MAIL ADDRESS _____

URL: http:// _____

KEYWORD _____

PHONE/FAX _____

NAME: GE Capital
URL: http://www.ge.com/gec/index.html

NAME: Get Organized
URL: http://www.get-organized.com

NAME: Global Business Network
URL: http://www.gbn.org

NAME: Global Trade Center
URL: http://www.tradezone.com/tz

NAME: GNN Personal Finance
URL: http://gnn.com/meta/finance

NAME: GNN Travel Center
URL: http://gnn-e2a.gnn.com/gnn/meta/travel/about.html

NAME: The Goodyear Tire and Rubber Company
URL: http://www.goodyear.com

NAME: Golf Channel
URL: http://www.gdol.com/golfchannel

NAME: Graphics and Desktop Publisher
URL: http://www.awa.com/nct/software/graplead.htm

NAME: Grolier Online
URL: http://www.grolier.com

NAME _____

E-MAIL ADDRESS _____

URL: http:// _____

KEYWORD _____

PHONE/FAX_____

NAME _____

E-MAIL ADDRESS _____

URL: http:// _____

KEYWORD _____

PHONE/FAX_____

NAME _____

E-MAIL ADDRESS _____

URL: http:// _____

KEYWORD _____

PHONE/FAX _____

NAME _____

E-MAIL ADDRESS _____

URL: http:// _____

KEYWORD _____

PHONE/FAX _____

NAME _____

E-MAIL ADDRESS _____

URL: http:// _____

KEYWORD _____

PHONE/FAX _____

NAME _____

E-MAIL ADDRESS _____

URL: http:// _____

KEYWORD _____

PHONE/FAX _____

NAME _____

E-MAIL ADDRESS _____

URL: http:// _____

KEYWORD _____

PHONE/FAX _____

NAME _____

E-MAIL ADDRESS _____

URL: http:// _____

KEYWORD _____

PHONE/FAX _____

NAME _____

E-MAIL ADDRESS _____

URL: http:// _____

KEYWORD _____

PHONE/FAX _____

NAME _____

E-MAIL ADDRESS _____

URL: http:// _____

KEYWORD _____

PHONE/FAX _____

NAME _____

E-MAIL ADDRESS _____

URL: http:// _____

KEYWORD _____

PHONE/FAX _____

NAME _____

E-MAIL ADDRESS _____

URL: http:// _____

KEYWORD _____

PHONE/FAX _____

NAME _____

E-MAIL ADDRESS _____

URL: http:// _____

KEYWORD _____

PHONE/FAX _____

NAME _____

E-MAIL ADDRESS _____

URL: http:// _____

KEYWORD _____

PHONE/FAX _____

NAME _____

E-MAIL ADDRESS _____

URL: http:// _____

KEYWORD _____

PHONE/FAX _____

NAME _____

E-MAIL ADDRESS _____

URL: http:// _____

KEYWORD _____

PHONE/FAX _____

NAME _____

E-MAIL ADDRESS _____

URL: http:// _____

KEYWORD _____

PHONE/FAX _____

NAME _____

E-MAIL ADDRESS _____

URL: http:// _____

KEYWORD _____

PHONE/FAX _____

NAME _____

E-MAIL ADDRESS _____

URL: http:// _____

KEYWORD _____

PHONE/FAX _____

NAME _____

E-MAIL ADDRESS _____

URL: http:// _____

KEYWORD _____

PHONE/FAX _____

NAME _____

E-MAIL ADDRESS _____

URL: http:// _____

KEYWORD _____

PHONE/FAX _____

NAME _____

E-MAIL ADDRESS _____

URL: http:// _____

KEYWORD _____

PHONE/FAX _____

NAME _____

E-MAIL ADDRESS _____

URL: http:// _____

KEYWORD _____

PHONE/FAX _____

NAME _____

E-MAIL ADDRESS _____

URL: http:// _____

KEYWORD _____

PHONE/FAX _____

NAME _____

E-MAIL ADDRESS _____

URL: http:// _____

KEYWORD _____

PHONE/FAX _____

NAME _____

E-MAIL ADDRESS _____

URL: http:// _____

KEYWORD _____

PHONE/FAX _____

NAME _____

E-MAIL ADDRESS _____

URL: http:// _____

KEYWORD _____

PHONE/FAX _____

NAME: HBO
URL: http://www.hbo.com

NAME: Hayes Microcomputer Products, Inc.
URL: http://www.hayes.com

NAME: HealthGate
URL: http://www.healthgate.com

NAME: Hemmings Motor News
URL: http://www.hmn.com

NAME: Hollywood Reporter
URL: http://www.hollywoodreporter.com

NAME: HomeOwners Finance Center
URL: http://www.homeowners.com/homeowners/index.html

NAME: Honda Motor Company
URL: http://www.honda.com

NAME: Honeywell Space & Aviation Control
URL: http://www.sac.honeywell.com

NAME: Hoover's Online
URL: http://www.hoovers.com

NAME: Hotel and Travel Index Online
URL: http://www.traveler.net/htio

NAME _____

E-MAIL ADDRESS _____

URL: http:// _____

KEYWORD _____

PHONE/FAX _____

NAME _____

E-MAIL ADDRESS _____

URL: http:// _____

KEYWORD _____

PHONE/FAX _____

NAME _____

E-MAIL ADDRESS _____

URL: http:// _____

KEYWORD _____

PHONE/FAX _____

NAME _____

E-MAIL ADDRESS _____

URL: http:// _____

KEYWORD _____

PHONE/FAX _____

NAME _____

E-MAIL ADDRESS _____

URL: http:// _____

KEYWORD _____

PHONE/FAX _____

NAME _____

E-MAIL ADDRESS _____

URL: http:// _____

KEYWORD _____

PHONE/FAX _____

NAME _____

E-MAIL ADDRESS _____

URL: http:// _____

KEYWORD _____

PHONE/FAX _____

NAME _____

E-MAIL ADDRESS _____

URL: http:// _____

KEYWORD _____

PHONE/FAX _____

NAME _____

E-MAIL ADDRESS _____

URL: http:// _____

KEYWORD _____

PHONE/FAX _____

NAME _____

E-MAIL ADDRESS _____

URL: http:// _____

KEYWORD _____

PHONE/FAX _____

NAME _____

E-MAIL ADDRESS _____

URL: http:// _____

KEYWORD _____

PHONE/FAX _____

NAME _____

E-MAIL ADDRESS _____

URL: http:// _____

KEYWORD _____

PHONE/FAX _____

NAME _____

E-MAIL ADDRESS _____

URL: http:// _____

KEYWORD _____

PHONE/FAX _____

NAME _____

E-MAIL ADDRESS _____

URL: http:// _____

KEYWORD _____

PHONE/FAX _____

NAME _____

E-MAIL ADDRESS _____

URL: http:// _____

KEYWORD _____

PHONE/FAX _____

NAME _____

E-MAIL ADDRESS _____

URL: http:// _____

KEYWORD _____

PHONE/FAX _____

NAME _____

E-MAIL ADDRESS _____

URL: http:// _____

KEYWORD _____

PHONE/FAX _____

NAME _____

E-MAIL ADDRESS _____

URL: http:// _____

KEYWORD _____

PHONE/FAX _____

NAME _____

E-MAIL ADDRESS _____

URL: http:// _____

KEYWORD _____

PHONE/FAX _____

NAME _____

E-MAIL ADDRESS _____

URL: http:// _____

KEYWORD _____

PHONE/FAX _____

NAME _____

E-MAIL ADDRESS _____

URL: http:// _____

KEYWORD _____

PHONE/FAX _____

NAME _____

E-MAIL ADDRESS _____

URL: http:// _____

KEYWORD _____

PHONE/FAX _____

NAME _____

E-MAIL ADDRESS _____

URL: http:// _____

KEYWORD _____

PHONE/FAX _____

NAME _____

E-MAIL ADDRESS _____

URL: http:// _____

KEYWORD _____

PHONE/FAX _____

NAME _____

E-MAIL ADDRESS _____

URL: http:// _____

KEYWORD _____

PHONE/FAX _____

NAME _____

E-MAIL ADDRESS _____

URL: http:// _____

KEYWORD _____

PHONE/FAX _____

NAME _____

E-MAIL ADDRESS _____

URL: http:// _____

KEYWORD _____

PHONE/FAX _____

NAME: IBM
URL: http://www.ibm.com

NAME: IndustryNET
URL: http://www.industry.net

NAME: Insurance Shopping Network
URL: http://www.800insureme.com

NAME: IntelliMatch Online Career Services
URL: http://www.intellimatch.com/intellimatch

NAME: International Cigar Club
URL: http://intpro.com/orlando/business/cigar/cigar1.html

NAME: Imperative!
URL: http://www.imperative.com/cgi-bin/genobject/index2

NAME: Internet Radio Nexus
URL: http://www.medium.com/IRT/ir1.html

NAME: Internet Resources Database
URL: http://www.internetdatabase.com/database.htm

NAME: Internic Whois
URL: http://rs.internic.net/cgi-bin/whois

NAME: InterQuote
URL: http://www.interquote.com

NAME _____

E-MAIL ADDRESS _____

URL: http:// _____

KEYWORD _____

PHONE/FAX _____

NAME _____

E-MAIL ADDRESS _____

URL: http:// _____

KEYWORD _____

PHONE/FAX _____

NAME _____

E-MAIL ADDRESS _____

URL: http:// _____

KEYWORD _____

PHONE/FAX _____

NAME _____

E-MAIL ADDRESS _____

URL: http:// _____

KEYWORD _____

PHONE/FAX _____

NAME _____

E-MAIL ADDRESS _____

URL: http:// _____

KEYWORD _____

PHONE/FAX _____

NAME _____

E-MAIL ADDRESS _____

URL: http:// _____

KEYWORD _____

PHONE/FAX _____

NAME _____

E-MAIL ADDRESS _____

URL: http:// _____

KEYWORD _____

PHONE/FAX _____

NAME _____

E-MAIL ADDRESS _____

URL: http:// _____

KEYWORD _____

PHONE/FAX _____

NAME _____

E-MAIL ADDRESS _____

URL: http:// _____

KEYWORD _____

PHONE/FAX _____

NAME _____

E-MAIL ADDRESS _____

URL: http:// _____

KEYWORD _____

PHONE/FAX _____

NAME _____

E-MAIL ADDRESS _____

URL: http:// _____

KEYWORD _____

PHONE/FAX _____

NAME _____

E-MAIL ADDRESS _____

URL: http:// _____

KEYWORD _____

PHONE/FAX _____

NAME _____

E-MAIL ADDRESS _____

URL: http:// _____

KEYWORD _____

PHONE/FAX _____

NAME _____

E-MAIL ADDRESS _____

URL: http:// _____

KEYWORD _____

PHONE/FAX _____

NAME _____

E-MAIL ADDRESS _____

URL: http:// _____

KEYWORD _____

PHONE/FAX _____

NAME _____

E-MAIL ADDRESS _____

URL: http:// _____

KEYWORD _____

PHONE/FAX _____

NAME _____

E-MAIL ADDRESS _____

URL: http:// _____

KEYWORD _____

PHONE/FAX _____

NAME _____

E-MAIL ADDRESS _____

URL: http:// _____

KEYWORD _____

PHONE/FAX _____

NAME _____

E-MAIL ADDRESS _____

URL: http:// _____

KEYWORD _____

PHONE/FAX _____

NAME _____

E-MAIL ADDRESS _____

URL: http:// _____

KEYWORD _____

PHONE/FAX _____

NAME _____

E-MAIL ADDRESS _____

URL: http:// _____

KEYWORD _____

PHONE/FAX _____

NAME _____

E-MAIL ADDRESS _____

URL: http:// _____

KEYWORD _____

PHONE/FAX _____

NAME _____

E-MAIL ADDRESS _____

URL: http:// _____

KEYWORD _____

PHONE/FAX _____

NAME _____

E-MAIL ADDRESS _____

URL: http:// _____

KEYWORD _____

PHONE/FAX _____

NAME _____

E-MAIL ADDRESS _____

URL: http:// _____

KEYWORD _____

PHONE/FAX _____

NAME _____

E-MAIL ADDRESS _____

URL: http:// _____

KEYWORD _____

PHONE/FAX _____

NAME _____

E-MAIL ADDRESS _____

URL: http:// _____

KEYWORD _____

PHONE/FAX _____

NAME: Jadco Stock Charts
URL: http://www.jadco.com

NAME: Jaguar Cars
URL: http://www.jaguarcars.com

NAME: Jazz Music Stores Around the World
URL: http://www.acns.nwu.edu/jazz/lists/stores.html

NAME: J.C. Penney
URL: http://www.jcpenney.com

NAME: Jeep
URL: http://www.jeepunpaved.com

NAME: Jerusalem Post
URL: http://www.jpost.co.il

NAME: JobBank USA
URL: http://www.jobbankusa.com

NAME: The Journal of Online Law
URL: http://www.law.cornell.edu/jol/jol.table.html

NAME: JUMBO! Shareware Archive
URL: http://www.jumbo.com

J

NAME: Juno (free e-mail)
URL: http://www.juno.com

NAME _____

E-MAIL ADDRESS _____

URL: http:// _____

KEYWORD _____

PHONE/FAX_____

NAME _____

E-MAIL ADDRESS _____

URL: http:// _____

KEYWORD _____

PHONE/FAX_____

NAME _____

E-MAIL ADDRESS _____

URL: http:// _____

KEYWORD _____

PHONE/FAX _____

NAME _____

E-MAIL ADDRESS _____

URL: http:// _____

KEYWORD _____

PHONE/FAX _____

NAME _____

E-MAIL ADDRESS _____

URL: http:// _____

KEYWORD _____

PHONF/FAX _____

NAME _____

E-MAIL ADDRESS _____

URL: http:// _____

KEYWORD _____

PHONE/FAX _____

NAME _____

E-MAIL ADDRESS _____

URL: http:// _____

KEYWORD _____

PHONE/FAX _____

NAME _____

E-MAIL ADDRESS _____

URL: http:// _____

KEYWORD _____

PHONE/FAX _____

NAME _____

E-MAIL ADDRESS _____

URL: http:// _____

KEYWORD _____

PHONE/FAX _____

NAME _____

E-MAIL ADDRESS _____

URL: http:// _____

KEYWORD _____

PHONE/FAX _____

NAME _____

E-MAIL ADDRESS _____

URL: http:// _____

KEYWORD _____

PHONE/FAX _____

NAME _____

E-MAIL ADDRESS _____

URL: http:// _____

KEYWORD _____

PHONE/FAX _____

NAME _____

E-MAIL ADDRESS _____

URL: http:// _____

KEYWORD _____

PHONE/FAX _____

NAME _____

E-MAIL ADDRESS _____

URL: http:// _____

KEYWORD _____

PHONE/FAX _____

NAME _____

E-MAIL ADDRESS _____

URL: http:// _____

KEYWORD _____

PHONE/FAX _____

NAME _____

E-MAIL ADDRESS _____

URL: http:// _____

KEYWORD _____

PHONE/FAX _____

NAME _____

E-MAIL ADDRESS _____

URL: http:// _____

KEYWORD _____

PHONE/FAX _____

NAME _____

E-MAIL ADDRESS _____

URL: http:// _____

KEYWORD _____

PHONE/FAX _____

NAME _____

E-MAIL ADDRESS _____

URL: http:// _____

KEYWORD _____

PHONE/FAX _____

NAME _____

E-MAIL ADDRESS _____

URL: http:// _____

KEYWORD _____

PHONE/FAX _____

NAME _____

E-MAIL ADDRESS _____

URL: http:// _____

KEYWORD _____

PHONE/FAX _____

NAME _____

E-MAIL ADDRESS _____

URL: http:// _____

KEYWORD _____

PHONE/FAX _____

NAME _____

E-MAIL ADDRESS _____

URL: http:// _____

KEYWORD _____

PHONE/FAX _____

NAME _____

E-MAIL ADDRESS _____

URL: http:// _____

KEYWORD _____

PHONE/FAX _____

NAME _____

E-MAIL ADDRESS _____

URL: http:// _____

KEYWORD _____

PHONE/FAX _____

NAME _____

E-MAIL ADDRESS _____

URL: http:// _____

KEYWORD _____

PHONE/FAX _____

NAME _____

E-MAIL ADDRESS _____

URL: http:// _____

KEYWORD _____

PHONE/FAX _____

NAME: Kamp, Henning–TV Satellite Stuff
URL: http://home.sol.no/hkamp/satellit.htm

NAME: KCBS–93 Los Angeles
URL: http://www.arrowfm.com

NAME: KDGE–94.5 Dallas/Fort Worth
URL: http://www.kdge.com/kdge

NAME: Kellogg's Cereal City
URL: http://www.kelloggs.com

NAME: Kia Motor Company
URL: http://www.kia.co.kr

NAME: Kinney Shoes
URL: http://www.kinney-shoes.com

NAME: Killersites (Creating Killer Websites)
URL: http://www.killersites.com

NAME: KISS Rocks–San Antonio
URL: http://www.kissrocks.com/index.html

NAME: Knowledge Industry Publications, Inc.
URL: http://www.KIPInet.com

NAME: Kongsberg Spacetec
URL: http://www.spacetec.no

K

NAME _____

E-MAIL ADDRESS _____

URL: http:// _____

KEYWORD _____

PHONE/FAX _____

NAME _____

E-MAIL ADDRESS _____

URL: http:// _____

KEYWORD _____

PHONE/FAX _____

NAME _____

E-MAIL ADDRESS _____

URL: http:// _____

KEYWORD _____

PHONE/FAX _____

NAME _____

E-MAIL ADDRESS _____

URL: http:// _____

KEYWORD _____

PHONE/FAX _____

NAME _____

E-MAIL ADDRESS _____

URL: http:// _____

KEYWORD _____

PHONE/FAX _____

NAME _____

E-MAIL ADDRESS _____

URL: http:// _____

KEYWORD _____

PHONE/FAX _____

NAME _____

E-MAIL ADDRESS _____

URL: http:// _____

KEYWORD _____

PHONE/FAX _____

NAME _____

E-MAIL ADDRESS _____

URL: http:// _____

KEYWORD _____

PHONE/FAX _____

NAME _____

E-MAIL ADDRESS _____

URL: http:// _____

KEYWORD _____

PHONE/FAX _____

NAME _____

E-MAIL ADDRESS _____

URL: http:// _____

KEYWORD _____

PHONE/FAX _____

NAME _____

E-MAIL ADDRESS _____

URL: http:// _____

KEYWORD _____

PHONE/FAX _____

NAME _____

E-MAIL ADDRESS _____

URL: http:// _____

KEYWORD _____

PHONE/FAX _____

NAME _____

E-MAIL ADDRESS _____

URL: http:// _____

KEYWORD _____

PHONE/FAX _____

NAME _____

E-MAIL ADDRESS _____

URL: http:// _____

KEYWORD _____

PHONE/FAX _____

NAME _____

E-MAIL ADDRESS _____

URL: http:// _____

KEYWORD _____

PHONE/FAX _____

NAME _____

E-MAIL ADDRESS _____

URL: http:// _____

KEYWORD _____

PHONE/FAX _____

NAME _____

E-MAIL ADDRESS _____

URL: http:// _____

KEYWORD _____

PHONE/FAX _____

NAME _____

E-MAIL ADDRESS _____

URL: http:// _____

KEYWORD _____

PHONE/FAX _____

NAME _____

E-MAIL ADDRESS _____

URL: http:// _____

KEYWORD _____

PHONE/FAX _____

NAME _____

E-MAIL ADDRESS _____

URL: http:// _____

KEYWORD _____

PHONE/FAX _____

NAME _____

E-MAIL ADDRESS _____

URL: http:// _____

KEYWORD _____

PHONE/FAX _____

NAME _____

E-MAIL ADDRESS _____

URL: http:// _____

KEYWORD _____

PHONE/FAX _____

NAME _____

E-MAIL ADDRESS _____

URL: http:// _____

KEYWORD _____

PHONE/FAX _____

NAME _____

E-MAIL ADDRESS _____

URL: http:// _____

KEYWORD _____

PHONE/FAX _____

NAME _____

E-MAIL ADDRESS _____

URL: http:// _____

KEYWORD _____

PHONE/FAX _____

NAME _____

E-MAIL ADDRESS _____

URL: http:// _____

KEYWORD _____

PHONE/FAX _____

NAME _____

E-MAIL ADDRESS _____

URL: http:// _____

KEYWORD _____

PHONE/FAX _____

NAME: Land Rover
URL: http://www.landrover.com

NAME: Learjet
URL: http://www.learjet.com

NAME: Lenscrafters
URL: http://www.lenscrafters.com

NAME: Levi Jeans
URL: http://www.levi.com

NAME: LEXIS-NEXIS Communication Center
URL: http://www.lexis-nexis.com

NAME: Lexus Automobiles
URL: http://www.lexususa.com

NAME: Library of Congress
URL: http://www.loc.gov

NAME: Lockheed Martin Corporation
URL: http://www.lmco.com

NAME: London Calling Internet
URL: http://www.demon.co.uk/london-calling

NAME: LucasArts Entertainment Company
URL: http://www.lucasarts.com

L

NAME _____

E-MAIL ADDRESS _____

URL: http:// _____

KEYWORD _____

PHONE/FAX _____

NAME _____

E-MAIL ADDRESS _____

URL: http:// _____

KEYWORD _____

PHONE/FAX _____

NAME _____

E-MAIL ADDRESS _____

URL: http:// _____

KEYWORD _____

PHONE/FAX _____

NAME _____

E-MAIL ADDRESS _____

URL: http:// _____

KEYWORD _____

PHONE/FAX _____

NAME _____

E-MAIL ADDRESS _____

URL: http:// _____

KEYWORD _____

PHONE/FAX _____

NAME _____

E-MAIL ADDRESS _____

URL: http:// _____

KEYWORD _____

PHONE/FAX _____

NAME _____

E-MAIL ADDRESS _____

URL: http:// _____

KEYWORD _____

PHONE/FAX _____

NAME _____

E-MAIL ADDRESS _____

URL: http:// _____

KEYWORD _____

PHONE/FAX _____

NAME _____

E-MAIL ADDRESS _____

URL: http:// _____

KEYWORD _____

PHONE/FAX _____

NAME _____

E-MAIL ADDRESS _____

URL: http:// _____

KEYWORD _____

PHONE/FAX _____

NAME _____

E-MAIL ADDRESS _____

URL: http:// _____

KEYWORD _____

PHONE/FAX _____

NAME _____

E-MAIL ADDRESS _____

URL: http:// _____

KEYWORD _____

PHONE/FAX _____

NAME _____

E-MAIL ADDRESS _____

URL: http:// _____

KEYWORD _____

PHONE/FAX _____

NAME _____

E-MAIL ADDRESS _____

URL: http:// _____

KEYWORD _____

PHONE/FAX _____

NAME _____

E-MAIL ADDRESS _____

URL: http:// _____

KEYWORD _____

PHONE/FAX _____

NAME _____

E-MAIL ADDRESS _____

URL: http:// _____

KEYWORD _____

PHONE/FAX _____

NAME _____

E-MAIL ADDRESS _____

URL: http:// _____

KEYWORD _____

PHONE/FAX _____

NAME _____

E-MAIL ADDRESS _____

URL: http:// _____

KEYWORD _____

PHONE/FAX _____

NAME _____

E-MAIL ADDRESS _____

URL: http:// _____

KEYWORD _____

PHONE/FAX _____

NAME _____

E-MAIL ADDRESS _____

URL: http:// _____

KEYWORD _____

PHONE/FAX _____

NAME _____

E-MAIL ADDRESS _____

URL: http:// _____

KEYWORD _____

PHONE/FAX _____

NAME _____

E-MAIL ADDRESS _____

URL: http:// _____

KEYWORD _____

PHONE/FAX _____

NAME _____

E-MAIL ADDRESS _____

URL: http:// _____

KEYWORD _____

PHONE/FAX _____

NAME _____

E-MAIL ADDRESS _____

URL: http:// _____

KEYWORD _____

PHONE/FAX _____

NAME _____

E-MAIL ADDRESS _____

URL: http:// _____

KEYWORD _____

PHONE/FAX _____

NAME _____

E-MAIL ADDRESS _____

URL: http:// _____

KEYWORD _____

PHONE/FAX _____

NAME _____

E-MAIL ADDRESS _____

URL: http:// _____

KEYWORD _____

PHONE/FAX _____

NAME: McDonnell Douglas Aircraft Corporation
URL: http://www.dac.mdc.com

NAME: MCI
URL: http://www.mci.com

NAME: Medaccess
URL: http://www.medacess.com

NAME: Media Central
URL: http://www.mediacentral.com

NAME: Mercedes-Benz of North America
URL: http://www.usa.mercedes-benz.com

NAME: Microsoft
URL: http://www.microsoft.com

NAME: MSNBC Interactive
URL: http://www.msnbc.com

NAME: MTV
URL: http://www.mtv.com

NAME: The Mutual Fund Cafe
URL: http://www.mfcafe.com

NAME: My Yahoo
URL: http://www.my.yahoo.com

M

NAME _____

E-MAIL ADDRESS _____

URL: http:// _____

KEYWORD _____

PHONE/FAX_____

NAME _____

E-MAIL ADDRESS _____

URL: http:// _____

KEYWORD _____

PHONE/FAX_____

NAME _____

E-MAIL ADDRESS _____

URL: http:// _____

KEYWORD _____

PHONE/FAX _____

NAME _____

E-MAIL ADDRESS _____

URL: http:// _____

KEYWORD _____

PHONE/FAX _____

NAME _____

E-MAIL ADDRESS _____

URL: http:// _____

KEYWORD _____

PHONE/FAX _____

NAME _____

E-MAIL ADDRESS _____

URL: http:// _____

KEYWORD _____

PHONE/FAX _____

NAME _____

E-MAIL ADDRESS _____

URL: http:// _____

KEYWORD _____

PHONE/FAX _____

NAME _____

E-MAIL ADDRESS _____

URL: http:// _____

KEYWORD _____

PHONE/FAX _____

NAME _____

E-MAIL ADDRESS _____

URL: http:// _____

KEYWORD _____

PHONE/FAX _____

NAME _____

E-MAIL ADDRESS _____

URL: http:// _____

KEYWORD _____

PHONE/FAX _____

NAME _____

E-MAIL ADDRESS _____

URL: http:// _____

KEYWORD _____

PHONE/FAX _____

NAME _____

E-MAIL ADDRESS _____

URL: http:// _____

KEYWORD _____

PHONE/FAX _____

NAME _____

E-MAIL ADDRESS _____

URL: http:// _____

KEYWORD _____

PHONE/FAX _____

NAME _____

E-MAIL ADDRESS _____

URL: http:// _____

KEYWORD _____

PHONE/FAX _____

NAME _____

E-MAIL ADDRESS _____

URL: http:// _____

KEYWORD _____

PHONE/FAX _____

NAME _____

E-MAIL ADDRESS _____

URL: http:// _____

KEYWORD _____

PHONE/FAX _____

NAME _____

E-MAIL ADDRESS _____

URL: http:// _____

KEYWORD _____

PHONE/FAX _____

NAME _____

E-MAIL ADDRESS _____

URL: http:// _____

KEYWORD _____

PHONE/FAX _____

NAME _____

E-MAIL ADDRESS _____

URL: http:// _____

KEYWORD _____

PHONE/FAX _____

NAME _____

E-MAIL ADDRESS _____

URL: http:// _____

KEYWORD _____

PHONE/FAX _____

NAME _____

E-MAIL ADDRESS _____

URL: http:// _____

KEYWORD _____

PHONE/FAX _____

NAME _____

E-MAIL ADDRESS _____

URL: http:// _____

KEYWORD _____

PHONE/FAX _____

NAME _____

E-MAIL ADDRESS _____

URL: http:// _____

KEYWORD _____

PHONE/FAX _____

NAME _____

E-MAIL ADDRESS _____

URL: http:// _____

KEYWORD _____

PHONE/FAX _____

NAME _____

E-MAIL ADDRESS _____

URL: http:// _____

KEYWORD _____

PHONE/FAX _____

NAME _____

E-MAIL ADDRESS _____

URL: http:// _____

KEYWORD _____

PHONE/FAX _____

NAME _____

E-MAIL ADDRESS _____

URL: http:// _____

KEYWORD _____

PHONE/FAX _____

NAME: National Locator & Data
URL: http://iu.net/hodges

NAME: National Public Radio
URL: http://www.npr.org

NAME: NetGuide Online
URL: http://techweb.cmp.com/techweb/ng/current

NAME: Netscape
URL: http://www.netscape.com

NAME: New Jersey Online
URL: http://www.nj.com

NAME: New York Daily News
URL: http://www.mostnewyork.com

NAME: New York Times
URL: http://www.nytimes.com

NAME: NewsTalk
URL: http://www.newstalk.com

NAME: Nick at Night
URL: http://nick-at-nite.viacom.com

NAME: Nissan
URL: http://www.nissanmotors.com

NAME _____

E-MAIL ADDRESS _____

URL: http:// _____

KEYWORD _____

PHONE/FAX _____

NAME _____

E-MAIL ADDRESS _____

URL: http:// _____

KEYWORD _____

PHONE/FAX _____

N

NAME _____

E-MAIL ADDRESS _____

URL: http:// _____

KEYWORD _____

PHONE/FAX _____

NAME _____

E-MAIL ADDRESS _____

URL: http:// _____

KEYWORD _____

PHONE/FAX _____

NAME _____

E-MAIL ADDRESS _____

URL: http:// _____

KEYWORD _____

PHONE/FAX _____

NAME _____

E-MAIL ADDRESS _____

URL: http:// _____

KEYWORD _____

PHONE/FAX _____

NAME _____

E-MAIL ADDRESS _____

URL: http:// _____

KEYWORD _____

PHONE/FAX _____

NAME _____

E-MAIL ADDRESS _____

URL: http:// _____

KEYWORD _____

PHONE/FAX _____

NAME _____

E-MAIL ADDRESS _____

URL: http:// _____

KEYWORD _____

PHONE/FAX _____

NAME _____

E-MAIL ADDRESS _____

URL: http:// _____

KEYWORD _____

PHONE/FAX _____

NAME _____

E-MAIL ADDRESS _____

URL: http:// _____

KEYWORD _____

PHONE/FAX _____

NAME _____

E-MAIL ADDRESS _____

URL: http:// _____

KEYWORD _____

PHONE/FAX _____

NAME _____

E-MAIL ADDRESS _____

URL: http:// _____

KEYWORD _____

PHONE/FAX _____

NAME _____

E-MAIL ADDRESS _____

URL: http:// _____

KEYWORD _____

PHONE/FAX _____

NAME _____

E-MAIL ADDRESS _____

URL: http:// _____

KEYWORD _____

PHONE/FAX _____

NAME _____

E-MAIL ADDRESS _____

URL: http:// _____

KEYWORD _____

PHONE/FAX _____

NAME _____

E-MAIL ADDRESS _____

URL: http:// _____

KEYWORD _____

PHONE/FAX _____

NAME _____

E-MAIL ADDRESS _____

URL: http:// _____

KEYWORD _____

PHONE/FAX _____

NAME _____

E-MAIL ADDRESS _____

URL: http:// _____

KEYWORD _____

PHONE/FAX _____

NAME _____

E-MAIL ADDRESS _____

URL: http:// _____

KEYWORD _____

PHONE/FAX _____

NAME _____

E-MAIL ADDRESS _____

URL: http:// _____

KEYWORD _____

PHONE/FAX _____

NAME _____

E-MAIL ADDRESS _____

URL: http:// _____

KEYWORD _____

PHONE/FAX _____

91

NAME _____

E-MAIL ADDRESS _____

URL: http:// _____

KEYWORD _____

PHONE/FAX _____

NAME _____

E-MAIL ADDRESS _____

URL: http:// _____

KEYWORD _____

PHONE/FAX _____

NAME _____

E-MAIL ADDRESS _____

URL: http:// _____

KEYWORD _____

PHONE/FAX _____

NAME _____

E-MAIL ADDRESS _____

URL: http:// _____

KEYWORD _____

PHONE/FAX _____

NAME _____

E-MAIL ADDRESS _____

URL: http:// _____

KEYWORD _____

PHONE/FAX _____

NAME: "Off The Record"
URL: http://www.mediapool.com/offtherecord

NAME: Offbeat Britain
URL: http://adsint.bc.ca/britain

NAME: Oil and Gas Journal
URL: http://www.ogj.com

NAME: The One-Stop Windows 95 Site
URL: http://www.win95.com

NAME: Online Career Center
URL: http://www.occ.com/occ/HomePage.html

NAME: On-Line Sextant (from *Outbound Travel Magazine*)
URL: http://www.outboundtrav.com/online.sextant.html

NAME: OPPortunity NETwork
URL: http://www.oppnet.com/ern

NAME: Oracle New Media Products
URL: http://www.oracle.com/products/media_net/html

NAME: Orbis Investment Management Limited
URL: http://www.orbis.bm

NAME: ORBIT
URL: http://www.pi.se/orbit/welcome.html

NAME _____

E-MAIL ADDRESS _____

URL: http:// _____

KEYWORD _____

PHONE/FAX _____

NAME _____

E-MAIL ADDRESS _____

URL: http:// _____

KEYWORD _____

PHONE/FAX _____

NAME _____

E-MAIL ADDRESS _____

URL: http:// _____

KEYWORD _____

PHONE/FAX _____

NAME _____

E-MAIL ADDRESS _____

URL: http:// _____

KEYWORD _____

PHONE/FAX _____

NAME _____

E-MAIL ADDRESS _____

URL: http:// _____

KEYWORD _____

PHONE/FAX _____

NAME _____

E-MAIL ADDRESS _____

URL: http:// _____

KEYWORD _____

PHONE/FAX _____

NAME _____

E-MAIL ADDRESS _____

URL: http:// _____

KEYWORD _____

PHONE/FAX _____

NAME _____

E-MAIL ADDRESS _____

URL: http:// _____

KEYWORD _____

PHONE/FAX _____

NAME _____

E-MAIL ADDRESS _____

URL: http:// _____

KEYWORD _____

PHONE/FAX _____

NAME _____

E-MAIL ADDRESS _____

URL: http:// _____

KEYWORD _____

PHONE/FAX _____

NAME _____

E-MAIL ADDRESS _____

URL: http:// _____

KEYWORD _____

PHONE/FAX _____

NAME _____

E-MAIL ADDRESS _____

URL: http:// _____

KEYWORD _____

PHONE/FAX _____

NAME _____

E-MAIL ADDRESS _____

URL: http:// _____

KEYWORD _____

PHONE/FAX _____

NAME _____

E-MAIL ADDRESS _____

URL: http:// _____

KEYWORD _____

PHONE/FAX _____

NAME _____

E-MAIL ADDRESS _____

URL: http:// _____

KEYWORD _____

PHONE/FAX _____

NAME _____

E-MAIL ADDRESS _____

URL: http:// _____

KEYWORD _____

PHONE/FAX _____

NAME _____

E-MAIL ADDRESS _____

URL: http:// _____

KEYWORD _____

PHONE/FAX _____

NAME _____

E-MAIL ADDRESS _____

URL: http:// _____

KEYWORD _____

PHONE/FAX _____

NAME _____

E-MAIL ADDRESS _____

URL: http:// _____

KEYWORD _____

PHONE/FAX _____

NAME _____

E-MAIL ADDRESS _____

URL: http:// _____

KEYWORD _____

PHONE/FAX _____

NAME _____

E-MAIL ADDRESS _____

URL: http:// _____

KEYWORD _____

PHONE/FAX _____

NAME _____

E-MAIL ADDRESS _____

URL: http:// _____

KEYWORD _____

PHONE/FAX _____

NAME _____

E-MAIL ADDRESS _____

URL: http:// _____

KEYWORD _____

PHONE/FAX _____

NAME _____

E-MAIL ADDRESS _____

URL: http:// _____

KEYWORD _____

PHONE/FAX _____

NAME _____

E-MAIL ADDRESS _____

URL: http:// _____

KEYWORD _____

PHONE/FAX _____

NAME _____

E-MAIL ADDRESS _____

URL: http:// _____

KEYWORD _____

PHONE/FAX _____

NAME _____

E-MAIL ADDRESS _____

URL: http:// _____

KEYWORD _____

PHONE/FAX _____

NAME: Packard Bell
URL: http://www.packardbell.com

NAME: Penguin USA
URL: http://www.penguin.com/usa

NAME: Plymouth
URL: http://www.plymouthcars.com

NAME: Pointcast
URL: http://www.pointcast.com

NAME: Politically Correct Bedtime Stories
URL: http://w3.macdigital.com/macdigital/pcbs

NAME: Porsche Cars of North America
URL: http://www.porsche-usa.com

NAME: Prentice Hall Direct
URL: http://www.phdirect.com

NAME: Prodigy International
URL: http://www.internationalink.com

NAME: Putnam Berkley Group, Inc.
URL: http://www.putnam.com/putnam

NAME: QVC
URL: http://www.qvc.com

NAME _____

E-MAIL ADDRESS_____

URL: http:// _____

KEYWORD _____

PHONE/FAX _____

P
Q

NAME _____

E-MAIL ADDRESS_____

URL: http:// _____

KEYWORD _____

PHONE/FAX _____

NAME _____

E-MAIL ADDRESS _____

URL: http:// _____

KEYWORD _____

PHONE/FAX _____

NAME _____

E-MAIL ADDRESS _____

URL: http:// _____

KEYWORD _____

PHONE/FAX _____

NAME _____

E-MAIL ADDRESS _____

URL: http:// _____

KEYWORD _____

PHONE/FAX _____

NAME _____

E-MAIL ADDRESS _____

URL: http:// _____

KEYWORD _____

PHONE/FAX _____

NAME _____

E-MAIL ADDRESS _____

URL: http:// _____

KEYWORD _____

PHONE/FAX _____

NAME _____

E-MAIL ADDRESS _____

URL: http:// _____

KEYWORD _____

PHONE/FAX _____

NAME _____

E-MAIL ADDRESS _____

URL: http:// _____

KEYWORD _____

PHONE/FAX _____

NAME _____

E-MAIL ADDRESS _____

URL: http:// _____

KEYWORD _____

PHONE/FAX _____

NAME _____

E-MAIL ADDRESS _____

URL: http:// _____

KEYWORD _____

PHONE/FAX _____

NAME _____

E-MAIL ADDRESS _____

URL: http:// _____

KEYWORD _____

PHONE/FAX _____

NAME _____

E-MAIL ADDRESS _____

URL: http:// _____

KEYWORD _____

PHONE/FAX _____

NAME _____

E-MAIL ADDRESS _____

URL: http:// _____

KEYWORD _____

PHONE/FAX _____

NAME _____

E-MAIL ADDRESS _____

URL: http:// _____

KEYWORD _____

PHONE/FAX _____

NAME _____

E-MAIL ADDRESS _____

URL: http:// _____

KEYWORD _____

PHONE/FAX _____

NAME _____

E-MAIL ADDRESS _____

URL: http:// _____

KEYWORD _____

PHONE/FAX _____

NAME _____

E-MAIL ADDRESS _____

URL: http:// _____

KEYWORD _____

PHONE/FAX _____

NAME _____

E-MAIL ADDRESS _____

URL: http:// _____

KEYWORD _____

PHONE/FAX _____

NAME _____

E-MAIL ADDRESS _____

URL: http:// _____

KEYWORD _____

PHONE/FAX _____

NAME _____

E-MAIL ADDRESS _____

URL: http:// _____

KEYWORD _____

PHONE/FAX _____

NAME _____

E-MAIL ADDRESS _____

URL: http:// _____

KEYWORD _____

PHONE/FAX _____

NAME _____

E-MAIL ADDRESS _____

URL: http:// _____

KEYWORD _____

PHONE/FAX _____

NAME _____

E-MAIL ADDRESS _____

URL: http:// _____

KEYWORD _____

PHONE/FAX _____

NAME _____

E-MAIL ADDRESS _____

URL: http:// _____

KEYWORD _____

PHONE/FAX _____

NAME _____

E-MAIL ADDRESS _____

URL: http:// _____

KEYWORD _____

PHONE/FAX _____

NAME _____

E-MAIL ADDRESS _____

URL: http:// _____

KEYWORD _____

PHONE/FAX _____

NAME: RadioClassics
URL: http://www.radioclassics.com

NAME: Raytheon Company
URL: http://www.raytheon.com

NAME: RealAudio
URL: http://www.realaudio.com

NAME: Real Estate Web
URL: http://www.infi.net/REWeb

NAME: Recent Ebert Movie Reviews
URL: http://www.suntimes.com/ebert

NAME: Rent Net
URL: http://www.rent.net

NAME: Rockwell International
URL: http://www.rockwell.com

NAME: Roget's Thesaurus
URL: http://www.thesaurus.com

NAME: RON–Recruiters Online Network
URL: http://www.ipa.com

NAME: Royal Caribbean
URL: http://www.royalcaribbean.com/royal/main.html

NAME _____

E-MAIL ADDRESS _____

URL: http:// _____

KEYWORD _____

PHONE/FAX _____

NAME _____

E-MAIL ADDRESS _____

URL: http:// _____

KEYWORD _____

PHONE/FAX _____

R

NAME _____

E-MAIL ADDRESS _____

URL: http:// _____

KEYWORD _____

PHONE/FAX _____

NAME _____

E-MAIL ADDRESS _____

URL: http:// _____

KEYWORD _____

PHONE/FAX _____

NAME _____

E-MAIL ADDRESS _____

URL: http:// _____

KEYWORD _____

PHONE/FAX _____

NAME _____

E-MAIL ADDRESS _____

URL: http:// _____

KEYWORD _____

PHONE/FAX _____

NAME _____

E-MAIL ADDRESS _____

URL: http:// _____

KEYWORD _____

PHONE/FAX _____

NAME _____

E-MAIL ADDRESS _____

URL: http:// _____

KEYWORD _____

PHONE/FAX _____

NAME _____

E-MAIL ADDRESS _____

URL: http:// _____

KEYWORD _____

PHONE/FAX _____

NAME _____

E-MAIL ADDRESS _____

URL: http:// _____

KEYWORD _____

PHONE/FAX _____

NAME _____

E-MAIL ADDRESS _____

URL: http:// _____

KEYWORD _____

PHONE/FAX _____

NAME _____

E-MAIL ADDRESS _____

URL: http:// _____

KEYWORD _____

PHONE/FAX _____

NAME _____

E-MAIL ADDRESS _____

URL: http:// _____

KEYWORD _____

PHONE/FAX _____

NAME _____

E-MAIL ADDRESS _____

URL: http:// _____

KEYWORD _____

PHONE/FAX _____

NAME _____

E-MAIL ADDRESS _____

URL: http:// _____

KEYWORD _____

PHONE/FAX _____

NAME _____

E-MAIL ADDRESS _____

URL: http:// _____

KEYWORD _____

PHONE/FAX _____

NAME _____

E-MAIL ADDRESS _____

URL: http:// _____

KEYWORD _____

PHONE/FAX _____

NAME _____

E-MAIL ADDRESS _____

URL: http:// _____

KEYWORD _____

PHONE/FAX _____

NAME _____

E-MAIL ADDRESS _____

URL: http:// _____

KEYWORD _____

PHONE/FAX _____

NAME _____

E-MAIL ADDRESS _____

URL: http:// _____

KEYWORD _____

PHONE/FAX _____

NAME _____

E-MAIL ADDRESS _____

URL: http:// _____

KEYWORD _____

PHONE/FAX _____

NAME _____

E-MAIL ADDRESS _____

URL: http:// _____

KEYWORD _____

PHONE/FAX _____

NAME _____

E-MAIL ADDRESS _____

URL: http:// _____

KEYWORD _____

PHONE/FAX _____

NAME _____

E-MAIL ADDRESS _____

URL: http:// _____

KEYWORD _____

PHONE/FAX _____

NAME _____

E-MAIL ADDRESS _____

URL: http:// _____

KEYWORD _____

PHONE/FAX _____

NAME _____

E-MAIL ADDRESS _____

URL: http:// _____

KEYWORD _____

PHONE/FAX _____

NAME _____

E-MAIL ADDRESS _____

URL: http:// _____

KEYWORD _____

PHONE/FAX _____

NAME: Saab
URL: http://www.saabusa.com

NAME: Saturn Cars
URL: http://www.saturncars.com

NAME: Sci-Fi Channel
URL: http://www.scifi.com

NAME: Smart Business Supersite
URL: http://www.smartbiz.com

NAME: Smart Wine Magazine
URL: http://smartwine.com/consumer/swmay96/sw596cnt.htm

NAME: Speedtraps
URL: http://www.speedtrap.com/speedtrap

NAME: Special Olympics Int.
URL: http://specialolympics.org

NAME: Sprint
URL: http://www.sprint.com

NAME: Strong Funds
URL: http://www.strong-funds.com

NAME: Switchboard
URL: http://www.switchboard.com

NAME _____

E-MAIL ADDRESS _____

URL: http:// _____

KEYWORD _____

PHONE/FAX _____

NAME _____

E-MAIL ADDRESS _____

URL: http:// _____

KEYWORD _____

PHONE/FAX _____

S

NAME _____

E-MAIL ADDRESS _____

URL: http:// _____

KEYWORD _____

PHONE/FAX _____

NAME _____

E-MAIL ADDRESS _____

URL: http:// _____

KEYWORD _____

PHONE/FAX _____

NAME _____

E-MAIL ADDRESS _____

URL: http:// _____

KEYWORD _____

PHONE/FAX _____

NAME _____

E-MAIL ADDRESS _____

URL: http:// _____

KEYWORD _____

PHONE/FAX _____

NAME _____

E-MAIL ADDRESS _____

URL: http:// _____

KEYWORD _____

PHONE/FAX _____

NAME _____

E-MAIL ADDRESS _____

URL: http:// _____

KEYWORD _____

PHONE/FAX _____

NAME _____

E-MAIL ADDRESS _____

URL: http:// _____

KEYWORD _____

PHONE/FAX _____

NAME _____

E-MAIL ADDRESS _____

URL: http:// _____

KEYWORD _____

PHONE/FAX _____

NAME _____

E-MAIL ADDRESS _____

URL: http:// _____

KEYWORD _____

PHONE/FAX _____

NAME _____

E-MAIL ADDRESS _____

URL: http:// _____

KEYWORD _____

PHONE/FAX _____

NAME _____

E-MAIL ADDRESS _____

URL: http:// _____

KEYWORD _____

PHONE/FAX _____

NAME _____

E-MAIL ADDRESS _____

URL: http:// _____

KEYWORD _____

PHONE/FAX _____

NAME _____

E-MAIL ADDRESS _____

URL: http:// _____

KEYWORD _____

PHONE/FAX _____

NAME _____

E-MAIL ADDRESS _____

URL: http:// _____

KEYWORD _____

PHONE/FAX _____

NAME _____

E-MAIL ADDRESS _____

URL: http:// _____

KEYWORD _____

PHONE/FAX _____

114

NAME _____

E-MAIL ADDRESS _____

URL: http:// _____

KEYWORD _____

PHONE/FAX _____

NAME _____

E-MAIL ADDRESS _____

URL: http:// _____

KEYWORD _____

PHONE/FAX _____

NAME _____

E-MAIL ADDRESS _____

URL: http:// _____

KEYWORD _____

PHONE/FAX _____

NAME _____

E-MAIL ADDRESS _____

URL: http:// _____

KEYWORD _____

PHONE/FAX _____

NAME _____

E-MAIL ADDRESS _____

URL: http:// _____

KEYWORD _____

PHONE/FAX _____

NAME _____

E-MAIL ADDRESS _____

URL: http:// _____

KEYWORD _____

PHONE/FAX _____

NAME _____

E-MAIL ADDRESS _____

URL: http:// _____

KEYWORD _____

PHONE/FAX _____

NAME _____

E-MAIL ADDRESS _____

URL: http:// _____

KEYWORD _____

PHONE/FAX _____

NAME _____

E-MAIL ADDRESS _____

URL: http:// _____

KEYWORD _____

PHONE/FAX _____

NAME _____

E-MAIL ADDRESS _____

URL: http:// _____

KEYWORD _____

PHONE/FAX _____

NAME: T. Rowe Price
URL: http://www.troweprice.com

NAME: Tandy Corporation
URL: http://www.tandy.com

NAME: Thomas Register Home Page
URL: http://www.thomasregister.com

NAME: Toyota OnLine
URL: http://www.toyota.com.au

NAME: Trade Show Central
URL: http://www.tscentral.com

NAME: Traders' Connection
URL: http://www.trader.com

NAME: Travel Channel
URL: http://www.travelchannel.com

NAME: Travel Source
URL: http://www.travelsource.com

NAME: TravelWeb
URL: http://www.travelweb.com

NAME: TRW
URL: http://www.trw.com

NAME _____

E-MAIL ADDRESS _____

URL: http:// _____

KEYWORD _____

PHONE/FAX _____

NAME _____

E-MAIL ADDRESS _____

URL: http:// _____

KEYWORD _____

PHONE/FAX _____

T

NAME _____

E-MAIL ADDRESS _____

URL: http:// _____

KEYWORD _____

PHONE/FAX _____

NAME _____

E-MAIL ADDRESS _____

URL: http:// _____

KEYWORD _____

PHONE/FAX _____

NAME _____

E-MAIL ADDRESS _____

URL: http:// _____

KEYWORD _____

PHONE/FAX _____

NAME _____

E-MAIL ADDRESS _____

URL: http:// _____

KEYWORD _____

PHONE/FAX _____

NAME _____

E-MAIL ADDRESS _____

URL: http:// _____

KEYWORD _____

PHONE/FAX _____

NAME _____

E-MAIL ADDRESS _____

URL: http:// _____

KEYWORD _____

PHONE/FAX _____

NAME _____

E-MAIL ADDRESS _____

URL: http:// _____

KEYWORD _____

PHONE/FAX _____

NAME _____

E-MAIL ADDRESS _____

URL: http:// _____

KEYWORD _____

PHONE/FAX _____

NAME _____

E-MAIL ADDRESS _____

URL: http:// _____

KEYWORD _____

PHONE/FAX _____

NAME _____

E-MAIL ADDRESS _____

URL: http:// _____

KEYWORD _____

PHONE/FAX _____

NAME _____

E-MAIL ADDRESS _____

URL: http:// _____

KEYWORD _____

PHONE/FAX _____

NAME _____

E-MAIL ADDRESS _____

URL: http:// _____

KEYWORD _____

PHONE/FAX _____

NAME _____

E-MAIL ADDRESS _____

URL: http:// _____

KEYWORD _____

PHONE/FAX _____

NAME _____

E-MAIL ADDRESS _____

URL: http:// _____

KEYWORD _____

PHONE/FAX _____

NAME _____

E-MAIL ADDRESS _____

URL: http:// _____

KEYWORD _____

PHONE/FAX _____

NAME _____

E-MAIL ADDRESS _____

URL: http:// _____

KEYWORD _____

PHONE/FAX _____

NAME _____

E-MAIL ADDRESS _____

URL: http:// _____

KEYWORD _____

PHONE/FAX _____

NAME _____

E-MAIL ADDRESS _____

URL: http:// _____

KEYWORD _____

PHONE/FAX _____

NAME _____

E-MAIL ADDRESS _____

URL: http:// _____

KEYWORD _____

PHONE/FAX _____

NAME _____

E-MAIL ADDRESS _____

URL: http:// _____

KEYWORD _____

PHONE/FAX _____

NAME _____

E-MAIL ADDRESS _____

URL: http:// _____

KEYWORD _____

PHONE/FAX _____

NAME _____

E-MAIL ADDRESS _____

URL: http:// _____

KEYWORD _____

PHONE/FAX _____

NAME _____

E-MAIL ADDRESS _____

URL: http:// _____

KEYWORD _____

PHONE/FAX _____

NAME _____

E-MAIL ADDRESS _____

URL: http:// _____

KEYWORD _____

PHONE/FAX _____

NAME _____

E-MAIL ADDRESS _____

URL: http:// _____

KEYWORD _____

PHONE/FAX _____

NAME: U.S. Department of Housing and Urban Development
URL: http://www.hud.gov

NAME: United States Intelligence Community
URL: http://www.odci.gov/ic

NAME: United States Postal Service
URL: http://www.usps.gov

NAME: United States Tax Code Online
URL: http://www.fourmilab.ch/ustax/ustax.html

NAME: Universal Pictures
URL: http://www.mca.com/universal_pictures

NAME: Upline Online
URL: http://www.uplineonline.com

NAME: UPS
URL: http://www.ups.com

NAME: Upside
URL: http://www.upside.com

NAME: Upstart Magazine
URL: http://www.faludi.com/upSTART

NAME: USA Today
URL: http://www.usatoday.com

NAME _____

E-MAIL ADDRESS _____

URL: http:// _____

KEYWORD _____

PHONE/FAX _____

NAME _____

E-MAIL ADDRESS _____

URL: http:// _____

KEYWORD _____

PHONE/FAX _____

NAME _____

E-MAIL ADDRESS _____

URL: http:// _____

KEYWORD _____

PHONE/FAX _____

NAME _____

E-MAIL ADDRESS _____

URL: http:// _____

KEYWORD _____

PHONE/FAX _____

NAME _____

E-MAIL ADDRESS _____

URL: http:// _____

KEYWORD _____

PHONE/FAX _____

NAME _____

E-MAIL ADDRESS _____

URL: http:// _____

KEYWORD _____

PHONE/FAX _____

NAME _____

E-MAIL ADDRESS _____

URL: http:// _____

KEYWORD _____

PHONE/FAX _____

NAME _____

E-MAIL ADDRESS _____

URL: http:// _____

KEYWORD _____

PHONE/FAX _____

NAME _____

E-MAIL ADDRESS _____

URL: http:// _____

KEYWORD _____

PHONE/FAX _____

NAME _____

E-MAIL ADDRESS _____

URL: http:// _____

KEYWORD _____

PHONE/FAX _____

NAME _____

E-MAIL ADDRESS _____

URL: http:// _____

KEYWORD _____

PHONE/FAX _____

NAME _____

E-MAIL ADDRESS _____

URL: http:// _____

KEYWORD _____

PHONE/FAX _____

NAME _____

E-MAIL ADDRESS _____

URL: http:// _____

KEYWORD _____

PHONE/FAX _____

NAME _____

E-MAIL ADDRESS _____

URL: http:// _____

KEYWORD _____

PHONE/FAX _____

NAME _____

E-MAIL ADDRESS _____

URL: http:// _____

KEYWORD _____

PHONE/FAX _____

NAME _____

E-MAIL ADDRESS _____

URL: http:// _____

KEYWORD _____

PHONE/FAX _____

NAME _____

E-MAIL ADDRESS _____

URL: http:// _____

KEYWORD _____

PHONE/FAX _____

NAME _____

E-MAIL ADDRESS _____

URL: http:// _____

KEYWORD _____

PHONE/FAX _____

NAME _____

E-MAIL ADDRESS _____

URL: http:// _____

KEYWORD _____

PHONE/FAX _____

NAME _____

E-MAIL ADDRESS _____

URL: http:// _____

KEYWORD _____

PHONE/FAX _____

NAME _____

E-MAIL ADDRESS _____

URL: http:// _____

KEYWORD _____

PHONE/FAX _____

NAME _____

E-MAIL ADDRESS _____

URL: http:// _____

KEYWORD _____

PHONE/FAX _____

NAME _____

E-MAIL ADDRESS _____

URL: http:// _____

KEYWORD _____

PHONE/FAX _____

NAME _____

E-MAIL ADDRESS _____

URL: http:// _____

KEYWORD _____

PHONE/FAX _____

NAME _____

E-MAIL ADDRESS _____

URL: http:// _____

KEYWORD _____

PHONE/FAX _____

NAME _____

E-MAIL ADDRESS _____

URL: http:// _____

KEYWORD _____

PHONE/FAX _____

NAME _____

E-MAIL ADDRESS _____

URL: http:// _____

KEYWORD _____

PHONE/FAX _____

NAME: The Vanguard Group
URL: http://www.vanguard.com

NAME: VDOnet
URL: http://www.vdo.net

NAME: VH1
URL: http://www.viacom.com/vh1

NAME: Victoria and Albert Museum
URL: http://www.vam.ac.uk

NAME: Virgin Atlantic Airlines
URL: http://www.fly.virgin.com/atlantic

NAME: Virtual Job Fair
URL: http://www.careerexpo.com

NAME: Virtual Vegas
URL: http://www.virtualvegas.com

NAME: Volkswagen
URL: http://www.vw.com

NAME: Volvo Cars of North America
URL: http://www.volvocars.com

NAME: Voyager Books
URL: http://www.voyagerco/com/interface/gallery.cgi

NAME _____

E-MAIL ADDRESS _____

URL: http:// _____

KEYWORD _____

PHONE/FAX _____

NAME _____

E-MAIL ADDRESS _____

URL: http:// _____

KEYWORD _____

PHONE/FAX _____

NAME _____

E-MAIL ADDRESS _____

URL: http:// _____

KEYWORD _____

PHONE/FAX _____

NAME _____

E-MAIL ADDRESS _____

URL: http:// _____

KEYWORD _____

PHONE/FAX _____

NAME _____

E-MAIL ADDRESS _____

URL: http:// _____

KEYWORD _____

PHONE/FAX _____

NAME _____

E-MAIL ADDRESS _____

URL: http:// _____

KEYWORD _____

PHONE/FAX _____

NAME _____

E-MAIL ADDRESS _____

URL: http:// _____

KEYWORD _____

PHONE/FAX _____

NAME _____

E-MAIL ADDRESS _____

URL: http:// _____

KEYWORD _____

PHONE/FAX _____

NAME _____

E-MAIL ADDRESS _____

URL: http:// _____

KEYWORD _____

PHONE/FAX _____

NAME _____

E-MAIL ADDRESS _____

URL: http:// _____

KEYWORD _____

PHONE/FAX _____

NAME _____

E-MAIL ADDRESS _____

URL: http:// _____

KEYWORD _____

PHONE/FAX _____

NAME _____

E-MAIL ADDRESS _____

URL: http:// _____

KEYWORD _____

PHONE/FAX _____

NAME _____

E-MAIL ADDRESS _____

URL: http:// _____

KEYWORD _____

PHONE/FAX _____

NAME _____

E-MAIL ADDRESS _____

URL: http:// _____

KEYWORD _____

PHONE/FAX _____

NAME _____

E-MAIL ADDRESS _____

URL: http:// _____

KEYWORD _____

PHONE/FAX _____

NAME _____

E-MAIL ADDRESS _____

URL: http:// _____

KEYWORD _____

PHONE/FAX _____

NAME _____

E-MAIL ADDRESS _____

URL: http:// _____

KEYWORD _____

PHONE/FAX _____

NAME _____

E-MAIL ADDRESS _____

URL: http:// _____

KEYWORD _____

PHONE/FAX _____

NAME _____

E-MAIL ADDRESS _____

URL: http:// _____

KEYWORD _____

PHONE/FAX _____

NAME _____

E-MAIL ADDRESS _____

URL: http:// _____

KEYWORD _____

PHONE/FAX _____

NAME _____

E-MAIL ADDRESS _____

URL: http:// _____

KEYWORD _____

PHONE/FAX _____

NAME _____

E-MAIL ADDRESS _____

URL: http:// _____

KEYWORD _____

PHONE/FAX _____

NAME _____

E-MAIL ADDRESS _____

URL: http:// _____

KEYWORD _____

PHONE/FAX _____

NAME _____

E-MAIL ADDRESS _____

URL: http:// _____

KEYWORD _____

PHONE/FAX _____

NAME _____

E-MAIL ADDRESS _____

URL: http:// _____

KEYWORD _____

PHONE/FAX _____

NAME _____

E-MAIL ADDRESS _____

URL: http:// _____

KEYWORD _____

PHONE/FAX _____

NAME _____

E-MAIL ADDRESS _____

URL: http:// _____

KEYWORD _____

PHONE/FAX _____

NAME: Wall Street Journal
URL: http://www.wsj.com

NAME: Wall Street Net
URL: http://www.netresource.com/wsn

NAME: Wall Street Online
URL: http://www.wso.com/wso

NAME: WCBS–88 New York
URL: http://www.newsradio88.com

NAME: Weather Channel
URL: http://www.weather.com/weather

NAME: Web Digest for Marketers
URL: http://www.wdfm.com

NAME: Welcome to Intel
URL: http://www.intel.com

NAME: The White House
URL: http://www.whitehouse.gov

NAME: Writers Guild of America
URL: http://www.wga.org

NAME: World Currency Exchange
URL: http://www.rubicon.com/passport/currency/currency.htm

NAME _____

E-MAIL ADDRESS _____

URL: http:// _____

KEYWORD _____

PHONE/FAX _____

NAME _____

E-MAIL ADDRESS _____

URL: http:// _____

KEYWORD _____

PHONE/FAX _____

NAME _____

E-MAIL ADDRESS _____

URL: http:// _____

KEYWORD _____

PHONE/FAX _____

NAME _____

E-MAIL ADDRESS _____

URL: http:// _____

KEYWORD _____

PHONE/FAX _____

NAME _____

E-MAIL ADDRESS _____

URL: http:// _____

KEYWORD _____

PHONE/FAX _____

NAME _____

E-MAIL ADDRESS _____

URL: http:// _____

KEYWORD _____

PHONE/FAX _____

NAME _____

E-MAIL ADDRESS _____

URL: http:// _____

KEYWORD _____

PHONE/FAX _____

NAME _____

E-MAIL ADDRESS _____

URL: http:// _____

KEYWORD _____

PHONE/FAX _____

NAME _____

E-MAIL ADDRESS _____

URL: http:// _____

KEYWORD _____

PHONE/FAX _____

NAME _____

E-MAIL ADDRESS _____

URL: http:// _____

KEYWORD _____

PHONE/FAX _____

NAME _____

E-MAIL ADDRESS _____

URL: http:// _____

KEYWORD _____

PHONE/FAX _____

NAME _____

E-MAIL ADDRESS _____

URL: http:// _____

KEYWORD _____

PHONE/FAX _____

NAME _____

E-MAIL ADDRESS _____

URL: http:// _____

KEYWORD _____

PHONE/FAX _____

NAME _____

E-MAIL ADDRESS _____

URL: http:// _____

KEYWORD _____

PHONE/FAX _____

NAME _____

E-MAIL ADDRESS _____

URL: http:// _____

KEYWORD _____

PHONE/FAX _____

NAME _____

E-MAIL ADDRESS _____

URL: http:// _____

KEYWORD _____

PHONE/FAX _____

NAME _____

E-MAIL ADDRESS _____

URL: http:// _____

KEYWORD _____

PHONE/FAX _____

NAME _____

E-MAIL ADDRESS _____

URL: http:// _____

KEYWORD _____

PHONE/FAX _____

NAME _____

E-MAIL ADDRESS _____

URL: http:// _____

KEYWORD _____

PHONE/FAX _____

NAME _____

E-MAIL ADDRESS _____

URL: http:// _____

KEYWORD _____

PHONE/FAX _____

NAME _____

E-MAIL ADDRESS _____

URL: http:// _____

KEYWORD _____

PHONE/FAX _____

NAME _____

E-MAIL ADDRESS _____

URL: http:// _____

KEYWORD _____

PHONE/FAX _____

NAME _____

E-MAIL ADDRESS _____

URL: http:// _____

KEYWORD _____

PHONE/FAX _____

NAME _____

E-MAIL ADDRESS _____

URL: http:// _____

KEYWORD _____

PHONE/FAX _____

NAME _____

E-MAIL ADDRESS _____

URL: http:// _____

KEYWORD _____

PHONE/FAX _____

NAME _____

E-MAIL ADDRESS _____

URL: http:// _____

KEYWORD _____

PHONE/FAX _____

NAME _____

E-MAIL ADDRESS _____

URL: http:// _____

KEYWORD _____

PHONE/FAX _____

NAME: The X Forms Library
URL: http://bragg.phys.uwm.edu/xforms

NAME: XVScan
URL: http://www.tummy.com/xvscan

NAME: Xenon Labs–The Interactive Currency Table
URL: http://www.xe.net/currency/table.htm

NAME: Yankee Traveler
URL: http://www.tiac.net/users/macgyver/ne.html

NAME: Yahoo! Computing
URL: http://www.zdnet.com/yahoocomputing

**X
Y
Z**

NAME: Your Company
URL: http://pathfinder.com/@@rafYpZCYKgAAQA7V/money/yourco

NAME: Zagat's
URL: http://www.pathfinder.com/Travel/Zagat/Dine/index.html

NAME: Ziff Davis
URL: http://www.zdnet.com

NAME: Zine Scene
URL: http://internet-plaza.net/zone/zinescene

NAME: Zircon X11 IRC Client
URL: http://catless.ncl.ac.uk/Programs/Zircon

NAME _____

E-MAIL ADDRESS _____

URL: http:// _____

KEYWORD _____

PHONE/FAX _____

NAME _____

E-MAIL ADDRESS _____

URL: http:// _____

KEYWORD _____

PHONE/FAX _____

NAME _____

E-MAIL ADDRESS _____

URL: http:// _____

KEYWORD _____

PHONE/FAX _____

NAME _____

E-MAIL ADDRESS _____

URL: http:// _____

KEYWORD _____

PHONE/FAX _____

NAME _____

E-MAIL ADDRESS _____

URL: http:// _____

KEYWORD _____

PHONE/FAX _____

NAME _____

E-MAIL ADDRESS _____

URL: http:// _____

KEYWORD _____

PHONE/FAX _____

NAME _____

E-MAIL ADDRESS _____

URL: http:// _____

KEYWORD _____

PHONE/FAX _____

NAME _____

E-MAIL ADDRESS _____

URL: http:// _____

KEYWORD _____

PHONE/FAX _____

NAME _____

E-MAIL ADDRESS _____

URL: http:// _____

KEYWORD _____

PHONE/FAX _____

NAME _____

E-MAIL ADDRESS _____

URL: http:// _____

KEYWORD _____

PHONE/FAX _____

NAME _____

E-MAIL ADDRESS _____

URL: http:// _____

KEYWORD _____

PHONE/FAX _____

NAME _____

E-MAIL ADDRESS _____

URL: http:// _____

KEYWORD _____

PHONE/FAX _____

NAME _____

E-MAIL ADDRESS _____

URL: http:// _____

KEYWORD _____

PHONE/FAX _____

NAME _____

E-MAIL ADDRESS _____

URL: http:// _____

KEYWORD _____

PHONE/FAX _____

NAME _____

E-MAIL ADDRESS _____

URL: http:// _____

KEYWORD _____

PHONE/FAX _____

NAME _____

E-MAIL ADDRESS _____

URL: http:// _____

KEYWORD _____

PHONE/FAX _____

NAME _____

E-MAIL ADDRESS _____

URL: http:// _____

KEYWORD _____

PHONE/FAX _____

NAME _____

E-MAIL ADDRESS _____

URL: http:// _____

KEYWORD _____

PHONE/FAX _____

NAME _____

E-MAIL ADDRESS _____

URL: http:// _____

KEYWORD _____

PHONE/FAX _____

NAME _____

E-MAIL ADDRESS _____

URL: http:// _____

KEYWORD _____

PHONE/FAX _____

NAME _____

E-MAIL ADDRESS _____

URL: http:// _____

KEYWORD _____

PHONE/FAX _____

NAME _____

E-MAIL ADDRESS _____

URL: http:// _____

KEYWORD _____

PHONE/FAX _____

NAME _____

E-MAIL ADDRESS _____

URL: http:// _____

KEYWORD _____

PHONE/FAX _____

NAME _____

E-MAIL ADDRESS _____

URL: http:// _____

KEYWORD _____

PHONE/FAX _____

NAME _____

E-MAIL ADDRESS _____

URL: http:// _____

KEYWORD _____

PHONE/FAX _____

NAME _____

E-MAIL ADDRESS _____

URL: http:// _____

KEYWORD _____

PHONE/FAX _____

NAME _____

E-MAIL ADDRESS _____

URL: http:// _____

KEYWORD _____

PHONE/FAX _____

NOTES

NOTES

NOTES

NOTES

NOTES

NOTES

NOTES